SIXTH EDITION

P9-CAM-596

INTRODUCTION TO
LEGAL NURSE
CONSULTING

VICKIE L. MILAZZO
RN, MSN, JD, Editor

vickie milazzo institute

To the awesome CLNC® consultants whose dramatic and unique success stories always inspire me in my vision to revolutionize nursing careers one RN at a time.

Introduction to
Legal Nurse Consulting
SIXTH EDITION

Copyright © 2002, 2003, 2006, 2008, 2011, 2015
by Vickie Milazzo Institute.

ISBN-13:   978-1-933216-68-9
Editor: Vickie L. Milazzo, RN, MSN, JD

Publisher: Vickie Milazzo Institute
             5615 Kirby Drive, Suite 425
             Houston, Texas 77005
             713.942.2200
             LegalNurse.com

Formerly titled: *CLNC® Success Stories*

Printed in the United States of America

Printed on acid free paper (∞).

Contents

iii

3 Imagine, Believe, Achieve Your New Life as a CLNC® Consultant

Take the Fast Track to Financial Freedom

5 Use Vickie's Proven Strategies for Your Own CLNC® Success

Triumph Over Any Personal Challenge

7 Make More Than a Living, Make a *Difference*

Success Story *Contributors*

Introduction

What Is a Certified Legal Nurse Consultant^{CM}?

A Certified Legal Nurse Consultant^{CM} is a registered nurse who uses existing expertise as a healthcare professional plus specialized legal nurse consultant training to consult on medical-related cases at fees of up to $150/hour. Certified Legal Nurse Consultants^{CM} work closely with the 1,687,830* attorneys in the U.S. as the nursing and healthcare system experts on the litigation team.

They can also consult with a wide range of organizations including insurance companies, pharmaceutical companies, hospitals and other medical-related organizations. A CLNC® consultant bridges that gap in the attorney's knowledge. While the attorney is the expert on legal issues, the

> "Vickie Milazzo crossed nursing with the law and created a new profession. Now she trains scores of legal nurse consultants."
> – *The New York Times*

*Reported by state bar associations to Vickie Milazzo Institute in 2014.

Certified Legal Nurse Consultant^CM is the expert on nursing, the healthcare system and its inner workings.

What Does a CLNC® Consultant Do?

Certified Legal Nurse Consultants^CM apply their knowledge and understanding of medical, nursing and health-related issues to make an attorney's job easier, more efficient and more effective. Certified Legal Nurse Consultants^CM can offer a wide array of services from interpreting medical records to preparing deposition questions. For a full list of the 30 services offered by CLNC® consultants see the Role of The Certified Legal Nurse Consultant^CM, page 237.

What Types of Cases Do Certified Legal Nurse Consultants^CM Work On?

From groundbreaking litigation to standard medical malpractice, Certified Legal Nurse Consultants^CM can work on a nearly unlimited range of cases. Medical malpractice, products liability, criminal and workers' compensation are just a few of the types of cases on which legal nurse consultants can provide valuable insight. These specially trained nurses can be the difference in winning or losing for an attorney. For a full list of the types of cases handled by CLNC® consultants see the Role of The Certified Legal Nurse Consultant^CM, page 237.

> *A Certified Legal Nurse Consultant^CM uses existing expertise to consult on medical-related cases at fees of up to $150/hr.*

> *Certified Legal Nurse Consultants^CM work closely with the 1,687,830* attorneys in the U.S. as the nursing and healthcare experts on the litigation team.*

Why Should I Become a Certified Legal Nurse Consultant^{CM}?

By becoming a Certified Legal Nurse Consultant^{CM} you are demonstrating that you have mastered a complex body of specialized knowledge beyond the nursing degree. Recognized nationally by attorneys, the CLNC® Certification enhances your credibility with attorneys and promotes excellence in the principles and practices of legal nurse consulting. You will also become a member of the largest legal nurse consulting association in the U.S., the *National Alliance of Certified Legal Nurse Consultants* (*NACLNC*®).

What Will I Learn During the CLNC® Certification Program?

Vickie Milazzo Institute's CLNC® Certification Program is the most comprehensive legal nurse consultant training available to registered nurses. Developed and perfected for over 33 years by Vickie and her team of legal nurse consulting experts, the CLNC® Certification Program covers 19 modules starting with The Role of the Certified Legal Nurse Consultant^{CM} (page 237) through Business Development Principles to help you setup and manage your legal nurse consulting business. You can view our entire comprehensive legal nurse consulting curriculum and learn more about the CLNC® Certification Program at LegalNurse.com.

Vickie Milazzo Institute's CLNC® Certification Program is the most comprehensive legal nurse consultant training available to registered nurses.

"You can view our entire comprehensive legal nurse consulting curriculum and learn more at LegalNurse. com."

We encourage you to watch the complete Module 1: The Role of the Certified Legal Nurse Consultant^{CM} video. To enroll in this free 3½-hour online video course visit LegalNurse.com/free-video. You'll experience The Role of the Certified Legal Nurse Consultant^{CM} from the CLNC® Certification Program first hand. Complete the free program and receive 4 contact hours FREE.

10 Things Nursing Taught You About Owning a Business

by Vickie L. Milazzo, RN, MSN, JD

You have contemplated becoming a Certified Legal Nurse Consultant, and may be wondering if, as a nurse, you're cut out to be an entrepreneur and own your own business. After all, none of us were born entrepreneurs. It's not like when we were born our moms asked, "Is it a boy or a girl? And the doctor said, "No... it's a little entrepreneur."

We often look to outside experts for guidance and when I started my legal nurse consulting business in 1982, I wished that nursing school had

We Are Nurses and We Can Do Anything!®

trained me better for managing a business. Nursing school didn't offer classes such as marketing, accounting or business management. I wasn't confident that my nursing education and nursing experience had in any way prepared me to own my own business. However, I soon recognized that nursing gave me most of the answers for successfully starting my legal nurse consulting business. I also quickly discovered that I was better trained as an RN than most MBAs are for the world of entrepreneurship. Here are 10 things nursing taught me well about owning a business.

Success Lesson 1
You Have the Power to Take Control of Your Nursing Career

We all know that patients heal faster when they take control of their health and practice healthy habits. Even the smallest positive action can give a patient a sense of control and empower the healing process. Placebos are proof that if a patient believes he can be healed, his body does the necessary work for him.

You too have the power to practice the healthy habits essential for taking control of your career destiny. Educate yourself about the necessary steps to achieve career health, including new career options like legal nurse consulting. Then take control of your career destiny by taking action on those steps.

Success Lesson 2
Don't Give in to Fear

As a nurse, you often treat different patients who have the same progressive disease, yet they experience dramatically different outcomes. We all have known patients who lived years after their predicted demise and other patients who should have lived but didn't because they gave up. The fact that so many elderly patients die within months of losing a spouse is a sound example of the mind-body connection. In almost every case, the patients who died too soon had given in to their fear.

As Frank Herbert said in *Dune* "Fear is the mind-killer." Fear can paralyze you and keep you from making decisions. There's also a mind-business connection that will influence the health of your business.

When I give in to fear, I become the biggest obstacle to my success. Practice mind control and exercise your mind daily for positive thinking. Shake off any lack of confidence and negative thinking. Don't let fear be the reason you don't live your career dreams.

Always remember the mindset of the patients who live and the patients who die. The good news is that in business as opposed to nursing, bad results usually aren't fatal.

"Fear can paralyze you. Practice mind control and exercise your mind daily for positive thinking."

If you can make life and death decisions and handle life-threatening emergencies, you really can do anything.

Success Lesson 3
Nurses Can Do Anything

If you can make life and death decisions in the middle of the night, heal sick patients and handle life-threatening emergencies as easily as you make your bed in the morning, you really can do anything – especially something as straightforward as starting a legal nurse consulting business. Whenever I face a business crisis, I remind myself, "I'm a nurse and nurses can do anything." I've repeated this same message to myself for every obstacle I've had to overcome in my business.

You can apply the nursing process to any business situation and challenge.

Success Lesson 4
The Nursing Process Is Your Friend

When I left hospital nursing to pursue my legal nurse consulting business full-time, I thought I could set aside the "nursing process" forever. I couldn't have been more wrong. Business requires that same process of assessment, diagnosis, planning, implementation and evaluation. Every medical-related case you get involved in as a legal nurse consultant requires you to assess the possibilities and needs, diagnose the problems, plan how to achieve the goals, implement the plan and evaluate the results.

Your nursing jobs have prepared you well. You can apply the nursing process to any business situation and challenge. You will thank your nursing instructors for this one. Every time you review a case, interview with an attorney or face a challenge, you will rely on the process they taught you. Today, thanks to the analysis powers I gained from the nursing process, I handle things easily and successfully that would have seemed impossible 33 years ago. Aside from drawing blood, almost none of your nursing experience will be wasted in business.

Success Lesson 5
Act Quickly and Decisively

As an RN you know that seconds make a difference in patient outcomes. You rarely have lots of time to ponder or brood over a clinical decision. Act as quickly and decisively in your CLNC® business as you do as a hospital nurse and you will seize the opportunities that slower peers miss out on.

Will you always be correct? No. Will you make mistakes? Yes. But one thing for sure, you'll never be paralyzed into inaction. Don't miss your chance to succeed. Act quickly and decisively to launch and grow your CLNC® business.

Success Lesson 6
What You Focus on Is Where You Yield Results

Nurses are often overwhelmed by short staffing, heavy caseloads and lack of support from hospital administration. Even the general public knows that working conditions

Act as quickly and decisively in your CLNC® business as you do as a hospital nurse and you will seize opportunities.

for RNs are worse than ever. We quickly learn to triage and focus on what we need to do to heal patients in this less-than-ideal environment. Nursing taught me that where I focus my time is where I yield results.

That skill comes in handy for Certified Legal Nurse Consultants^CM. It's as important to triage and prioritize your actions in your CLNC® business as it is when working with patients. Every day I'm confronted with dozens of challenges, five things that must be done at once, and 20 new creative ideas for my business, but I rarely panic. The organizational and multitasking skills I learned as a nurse have served me well. When you start your CLNC® business, you will not receive any extra hours in the day. In fact, the days will feel shorter because you'll be enjoying your newfound freedom. Your ability to focus on what's really important is the perfect training for your successful CLNC® business.

Success Lesson 7
This Is Just Business, It's Not Cancer

Ministering to patients and family members helps nurses put life, with all its problems and challenges, into perspective. Today when I overreact to a problem or feel I'm in crisis, I think of sick and dying patients. I think, "Now fighting for your life is a REAL problem."

In business I've had lots of ups and downs. When the down moments come, I remind myself, "This is business – not cancer." This helps me focus positively on solving the problem rather than embarking on a pity party. I've thrown plenty of those "parties," and not only did they not make me feel any better, they never helped me solve a single business problem. As you grow your CLNC® business, it helps to ask, "So what if that one attorney says no?" or "So what if my favorite attorney-client retires?" and to remember it's just business, not cancer.

Success Lesson 8
Illness Can Wake You Up

All nurses have treated some patients who only began to live after they almost died. We've all had patients who said they are glad they got sick, because while they were well, they weren't living the life they wanted. The health crisis forced them to wake up, reassess their lives, decide what was truly important to them and go for it.

If your career is facing a health crisis, this is your opportunity to wake up and change things for the better. Today at work, ask yourself whether your nursing career is healthy and whether your nursing career is affecting your health and well-being. Wake up and remember that there's always time to make a change for the better – but it's better to do it now while you can still enjoy the change!

There's always time to make a change for the better – but it's better to do it now while you can still enjoy the change!

Success Lesson 9
Business Is Personal

Even though technical skills are vital for nurses, the relationships with patients and their families are usually what matters most. Those relationships pay off. When I was a young nurse, I made a mistake on one of my patients and he knew it. To my surprise the patient requested that I continue to be his nurse despite my error. I attributed his continuing trust to the relationship we had established together.

Just like nursing, business is personal. I have all the technical skills to lead my seminars and run my business. In fact, at this stage I could hand off some of those responsibilities to others. But I still teach every CLNC® Live Certification Program we offer and speak to students daily because those relationships are what I thrive on. No one else could replicate my relationship with each and every nurse. As a result, most of our business comes from referrals by practicing CLNC® consultants and graduates of Vickie Milazzo Institute.

Legal nurse consulting is a service business where you will apply the same relationship principles you learned in nursing to your attorney-clients and prospects. Provide quality service and excellent work product that no other legal nurse consultant can replicate, and soon you'll feel like you're in a short-staffing situation all over again.

Success Lesson 10
Take a Deep Breath When
Managing Your Employees

One more thing I learned, it's easier to manage an ICU full of patients than a room full of employees! At least you can sedate your patients.

Every lesson I learned from nursing, I apply to my business today. You've already learned similar lessons yourself. Take a moment to revel in everything nursing has taught you. These 10 Success Lessons will help you manifest any dream you desire, including becoming a CLNC® consultant.

These 10 Success Lessons will help you manifest any dream you desire, including becoming a CLNC® consultant.

A Day in the Life of a Certified Legal *Nurse* Consultant^{CM}

I Love the Benefits of a Highly Flexible Schedule

by Dorene Goldstein, RNC, BSN, CLNC, Massachusetts

> *My days are flexible. Some days I choose not to log any hours at all and relax by the pool.*

What I like best about being a Certified Legal Nurse Consultant^{CM} is the flexible schedule. I do not have a typical day or week for that matter. My days are flexible depending on what I need to get done. Some days I choose not to log any hours at all and relax by the pool, while other days I start at 9:00am sitting in my home office working on cases.

I usually sit and work for about two hours at a time and then I take a break.

During my break I either walk away completely from my office or I switch tasks. I love being able to have control over my schedule and to manage my time flexibly. Sometimes I work on many different cases at a time. If I get bored with research, I can work on a chronology or a case screening. This work is perfect for me as I like to keep it interesting. Since I never miss a meal, lunchtime comes quickly and I usually eat at about 12:30pm. I allow an hour for lunch and take the dog for a walk no matter what the weather is outside. This time helps clear my head – I find that when I go back to work after this break, I am extremely productive. Such is the benefit of having a very flexible schedule as a legal nurse consultant!

The afternoon is when I am usually at my best. I finish many tasks and check them off the list. This is a satisfying experience. While I would like to say that my days end at 4:00pm, this is usually not the case. I find that many nights after dinner, I return to my home office to plan out my week. Relax, I don't work every day of the week like this. Some days I only work in the afternoon or I don't put in any hours at all! My days and weeks are truly flexible and I can thank Vickie for that.

Working from home can certainly be a challenge for someone like me who gets distracted easily. Walking down the stairs to my office, I pass by the piles of laundry. When I put the laundry in the dryer, I have to take the other clothes out. When

> *I work on many different cases at a time. If I get bored with research, I can work on a chronology.*

> *This work is perfect for me.*

I put them away, I realize that the bed needs to be made, etc. The way I avoid this issue is to not do laundry or any other chores during my work day. If I work outside by the pool, this is never a problem because I can't see the housework that needs to be done.

My days and weeks are truly flexible and I can thank Vickie for that.

There's No Such Thing as a Typical Day for a CLNC® Consultant

by Jane A. Hurst, RN, CLNC, Ohio

One of the best parts about being a Certified Legal Nurse Consultant^CM is that my days are never the same. I enjoy the variety of my CLNC business and the ability to work when I want to.

I don't have set office hours. It's not because I'm a rebel – it's because I have attorney-clients in different time zones. I may have to speak with an attorney at 5:00am or at 8:00pm, but that is where my flexibility comes in.

I like to get up early. I'll have my coffee on the patio while I check the emails that came in overnight. One of my attorney-clients is six hours ahead of me, so he starts his work day in the middle of my night.

I then move into my home office to start working on cases. I am so lucky to have an actual office in my home. Before we moved here, I worked at my dining room table. It worked out pretty well since we rarely used the dining room. I kept a tablecloth folded up on one of the chairs. If someone stopped by unexpectedly, I would do my "reverse tablecloth trick" and throw it over the medical records that were strewn on top of the table. I still take over the dining room table when I have a case with voluminous records, but thankfully it's not my office desk anymore.

Most of the medical records I receive are sent to me electronically. The attorneys email them in pdf files or send a link to their internal network or a cloud server where I can access them for a certain period of time. I love using the next best thing, but there is one thing that I hold out on. I still like paper when reviewing medical records as a Certified Legal Nurse Consultant^{CM}. I like working with those 8½"x11" pieces of pulp fiber. It's not that I'm not capable of working with the records on my computer (Tom would be proud of me – I am set up with dual monitors). I have it set up so my cursor flows from one screen to the other seamlessly. I can highlight the important pieces of data on a page as well as any CLNC® consultant. I need to be able to sort, mark, highlight and otherwise fondle each page of the medical record. I guess it's just the way my brain processes information.

Needless to say, I have large quantities of paper. I have a lot of boxes of medical records which I keep for five years after the cases settle or go to trial. I use Microsoft® Office calendar to enter two dates. I enter a date one month before the records can be destroyed and the actual destroy date. When the first date rolls around, I contact the attorney who handled the case. I let him know I am going to be purging the records and ask if there is any need to retain them. If the answer is no I destroy

One of the best parts about being a Certified Legal Nurse Consultant^{CM} is that my days are never the same.

I enjoy the ability to work when I want to.

*There is no such thing as a typical day as a Certified Legal Nurse Consultant*CM *in a rural area, and that is exactly the way I like it!*

the records. Twice a year, I use a mobile shredding service. They come to my house and shred all of the documents I need destroyed. I look forward to shredding days. It clears out some space in the basement for a while.

Because I live in a rural area, most of my attorney-clients are in other cities and states. I have clients who I've worked with for years that I have never met face-to-face. Everything is handled remotely. Even the attorney-clients I have who are within driving distance, opt to mail or email the medical records. I Skype, speak with them on the phone or email to discuss cases.

As you can see, there is no such thing as a typical day as a Certified Legal Nurse ConsultantCM in a rural area, and that is exactly the way I like it!

The Best Part of Being a CLNC® Consultant Is Choosing How to Spend My Day

by Suzanne E. Arragg, RN, BSN, CDONA/LTC, CLNC, California

> *The BEST part is the ability to choose how to spend my day.*

The BEST part of being a Certified Legal Nurse Consultant^{CM} is the ability to choose how I want to spend my day. Barring the fact that there are times when I do not have the liberty to control my schedule because of an arbitration, mediation or trial, my typical day always begins with two cups of java while looking out onto my garden. Enjoying the quiet and tranquility of the morning keeps me centered and calm.

Once I have breakfast, I stroll into my home office and start checking email. Usually there are urgent requests from various attorney-clients on different medical-related cases, so I begin by prioritizing the order in which I need to respond. Then, I turn to the current project at hand. The project may be medical record review and analysis, reviewing a CLNC® subcontractor's latest report, reading deposition transcripts, reviewing medical bills, preparing a damages analysis and/or conducting research.

> *I am able to check email, enter billables and review the calendar – all while dinner is cooking!*

Soon it is time for lunch. Depending upon how busy the day is, I consume some healthy protein and then go for a 3-mile run. I clean up, grab a healthy snack and return to my home office to check email and resume the project at hand. Before I know it, it's time for dinner. I return to my kitchen where I prepare dinner for my family. Cooking is so therapeutic, rewarding and a great diversion from medical record review. Plus, I am able to check email, enter billables and review the next day's calendar – all while dinner is cooking! Once dinner is ready, we relax with a healthy glass of red wine, toast to a productive day and enjoy our meal.

There are occasions when a deadline is pressing and I return to my home office after dinner to work for a couple of hours, but it is reassuring that my attorney-clients continue to send work to me, so it's a good problem to have.

Sometimes the routine becomes mundane and I feel the need to change it up. On these days, I take a drive to the beach, go for a walk on the sand and then work the latter part of the day and early evening.

If this routine sounds too good to be true, it's not! It is truly representative of a day as a Certified Legal Nurse Consultant[CM]. There are days riddled with unexpected, atypical projects, and there are several days a month when I am traveling for various cases. Because today's technology allows quick access to information, I am able to meet my attorney-clients needs on the fly. At the end of every day, I toast to the awesomeness of being my own boss and my CLNC® success!

> *Every day, I toast to the awesomeness of being my own boss and my CLNC® success!*

*As a Certified Legal Nurse Consultant*CM*, my days are typically filled with interesting cases and attorney-clients, healthy exercise and the ability to work as hard as I want... or not!*

Each Day Is My Own as a Certified Legal Nurse Consultant*CM*

by Susan Schaab, RN, BSN, CLNC, Montana

For more than 20 years I worked as a staff nurse, and although the type of facility and specialty changed many times, the work did not. Every day I had a narrow window of time when I was allowed to clock in or out. I am habitually on time (meaning I have to get to work about 10-15 minutes early or I am late), so periodically I would get a reprimand for clocking in too early. Then there was the constant scrambling and juggling to complete my work and documentation or be dinged for too much overtime. Somewhere along the line, I managed to stay organized and punctual while delivering great patient care, but the fun of nursing would always be sapped from my job. Then I found Vickie and my life as a Certified Legal Nurse Consultant*CM*.

As my own boss, I never get reprimanded for getting to work too early, putting in too many hours on cases or building my CLNC® business. I can work, or not work, as my case load requires. Although I do stay organized and try to maintain a daily schedule, each day is gloriously flexible and my own!

As menopause starts, and sleeping is sometimes uncomfortable (hot flashes under thick Montana blankets are never pleasant), I occasionally find myself researching cases at strange hours. The Internet is always open and accessible, and surfing for new articles is really fun at 3:00am. The flexibility I have as a legal nurse consultant is amazing. I save my research in a reading list and dive into them later (it is easier to do a serious analysis in daylight). Several of my female attorney-clients understand this as I have received a few emails from them at around 2:00am. No, I don't answer until later as that could lead to some groggy conversations. It always makes me smile to think I am earning $125/hr in my pjs in the middle of the night.

My peak productivity hours are saved for case analysis and report writing. I crank up Pandora® for background music (no lyrics since singing along to 90s pop tends to send me off track and off key!) and can easily put in three to five hours without moving from my chair. After seven years as a Certified Legal Nurse Consultant^{CM} I am still amazed at how easy and enjoyable consulting with attorneys is. I get lost in my cases and am energized by them. I never felt that energy at the hospital unless it was an adrenaline rush from a delivery going bad, which was exciting but never fun. The flexibility that legal nurse consulting affords me is truly a blessing.

I find that exercise is important to relieve my aching butt muscles and get my juices flowing

> *As my own boss, each day is gloriously flexible and my own!*

> *It always makes me smile to think I am earning $125/hr in my pjs in the middle of the night.*

again, so early afternoon is my time to get outside or go to the gym. I take a couple of hours daily to hike, run or ski in the mountains.

Montana has short, amazingly beautiful summers and everyone is outside hiking, biking, running, fishing and hunting. I invested in high-end exercise gear because Vickie taught me to always look my best. As Vickie says, "You never know when or where you'll meet an attorney." One benefit of living in a small town is that I frequently see my attorney-clients. I have had many impromptu meetings while on a bike, or while training for a 10K. Recently two of these meetings brought me my most recent case.

As a Certified Legal Nurse Consultant[CM] my workstyle is completely flexible and completely my own. My days are typically filled with interesting cases and attorney-clients, healthy exercise and the ability to work as hard as I want… or not!

I Can't Imagine Doing Anything Else

by Dale Barnes, RN, MSN, PHN, CLNC, California

> *I never have a boring day or one in which I can predict exactly what will come my way.*

> *I love the challenge and can't imagine doing anything else.*

O ne of the things I love about being a Certified Legal Nurse Consultant^{CM} is no two days are alike. I am never bored and I always have to be on my toes, as I do not know what the day will have in store for me.

To elaborate on what some days are like, I've been working on a huge obstetrical case involving premature twins. The medical records are voluminous and I've spent days just organizing ten large binders of medical records. The way the records arrived was unbelievable. It was like someone had taken seven years worth of records, thrown them in the air and shuffled them. Those were not the most exciting days.

In the middle of tediously organizing medical records, I had fun going to a defense medical exam (DME) for the twins. I got to interact, play with them and have fun observing them. They are now seven years old, and quite rambunctious. Since the DME was about an hour-and-half drive from where I live, that was the bulk of my day. (And yes, I do charge for travel time).

In the midst of working on this bad baby case, I got a bad faith insurance case and a long term care case. I also got several complaints to review for the Board of Registered Nursing.

One day, I was reviewing a case in which I was to testify two weeks later. The case was one that originated as a complaint to the Board of Registered Nursing but had progressed to a lawsuit in which the issue was rescinding a nursing license. As I was preparing my testimony, the phone rang. It was an attorney I did not know. He had been referred to me by another Certified Legal Nurse Consultant[CM]. He told me he had a trial coming up in a couple of weeks and needed an expert quickly. He said the case involved defending a registered nurse to prevent rescinding of his license. I asked about the case to ensure there was no conflict of interest. Turns out I had to tell him this was the same case in which I was preparing to testify for the District Attorney. He asked if I could find him another nurse to testify. I told him I would be a bit uncomfortable finding someone I know to testify against me. I also told him I knew we could not discuss the case, but had to ask him if he had watched the videos that were presented as evidence in this case. His response was, "Yes, and I wish I was on your side!"

The above call came to me on a Friday. On Monday I got a call from another new attorney. He had a possible case involving a 12-year-old with a chronic condition. He was trying to decide whether to pursue just a negligence theory, or also include

I had fun going to a defense medical exam for twins. I got to play with them.

The DME was about an hour-and-half drive. (And yes, I do charge for travel time).

assault and battery because an MRI with sedation was given without parental consent. So, all those medical records were sent to me and I began my review.

In between all of the above, I was busy writing interrogatories and deposition questions for other cases that were in the discovery phase.

As you can see, I never have a boring day or one in which I can predict exactly what will come my way. I love the challenge and can't imagine doing anything else.

I got a call from another new attorney. He had a case involving a 12-year-old. So, all those records were sent to me.

Imagine, Believe, Achieve Your New *Life* as a CLNC® Consultant

A $1,000,000 Legal Nurse Consulting Business Is Attainable. Go for It – I Did

by Suzanne E. Arragg, RN, BSN, CDONA/LTC, CLNC, California

> *This was the most rewarding experience of my whole nursing career.*

I have been a registered nurse since 1985, but seven years ago my path began a slow and steady 180-degree turn. I'd been the director of nursing services in a skilled nursing facility (SNF) for just under a year, when my dad spotted a classified ad in our local newspaper. A defense law

I was so impacted by this experience I was convinced this was my future and a way to earn enough income to get out of debt.

firm was seeking a legal nurse consultant. I learned that this firm was legal counsel for three of the top five long term care corporations in the country. My initial response was, "I don't have that kind of training."

My director position included being on call 24 hours per day, 7 days a week. Besides this grueling job, I was going through a nasty divorce and had primary custody of my three children, ages 4, 6 and 8, with no child support. To top it off, I found out I needed a hysterectomy for a pre-cancerous condition.

I was depressed, sleep-deprived, stressed, short-tempered, financially upside-down and in debt. A financial advisor told me there was no way I could retire, even with Social Security. I felt like I was on a sinking ship.

Three weeks after my dad showed me the ad, I submitted my resume. I figured I had nothing to lose, and it's always good to keep my interviewing skills fresh. My SNF colleagues saw the same ad and submitted their resumes, too.

My Persistence Landed Me My First Assignment

I knew consistent follow-up was a must, once you have submitted a resume. Over the next five weeks, I had many pleasant conversations with the chief partner's legal secretary. I got to know her on a first-name basis, and she told me he was in trial and to keep calling. I also left voice mail messages for the attorney. Finally, he called me.

Obviously, he knew I was persistent, and at the first interview he could tell I presented well and I had the knowledge he needed to litigate his cases. Within a half-hour, we agreed on my hourly rate, which was more than I was then making, and I left with my first long term care case. Needless to say, my colleagues never got a call and were shocked at my success, especially since they had 15 years' experience on me.

This first case was voluminous – more than 30,000 pages of medical records spanning 20 years. I worked with the chief partner and one of his associates through the entire legal process. My tasks included organizing, reconstructing and analyzing the medical records, defining standards of nursing care, identifying state and federal regulatory deficiencies, identifying appropriate testifying experts, educating the attorney, assisting with trial preparation, and developing and designing demonstrative evidence used in the trial, just to name a few.

This was the most rewarding experience of my whole nursing career. I was intellectually challenged, and there was nothing mundane about the medical-legal process. I was so impacted by this experience I was convinced this was my future and a way to earn enough income to get out of debt. With my parents' support, I attended Vickie's CLNC® Certification Seminar and became a Certified Legal Nurse Consultant℠.

The day I got home from the seminar, I called my attorney-client, who had just received the jury

We had won this landmark case and he was absolutely thrilled. He couldn't thank me enough.

Vickie is incredibly motivating. She knows how to speak to a nurse's heart.

verdict: We had won this landmark case. I was ecstatic and he was absolutely thrilled. He couldn't thank me enough for educating and assisting him with my nursing expertise. He said he would refer all his cases to me. I thanked him profusely and informed him of my new CLNC® status. He became a very high-volume client for me.

My CLNC® Certification Made All the Difference in My Full-Time Success

Vickie's CLNC® Certification Program and *Core Curriculum for Legal Nurse Consulting*® textbook expanded my limited understanding of the legal nurse consultant's role. They helped me improve my reports and presentation style, and provided me with the business strategies needed to become an independent business owner, not to mention the tools needed to build a million-dollar business.

Vickie is incredibly motivating. She knows how to speak to a nurse's heart. Her endless energy emanates through her words. Throughout the CLNC® Certification Seminar, I could see she was totally engrossed in what she was teaching. I identified with passion, but I also realized I didn't exhibit passion like she did. I made a commitment to express my passion as Vickie does and maintain an upbeat and positive attitude in my life and in my business. This attitude encourages my attorney-clients as well. You make a better overall impression by always appearing confident, cheerful and optimistic. This helps keep your clients happy and

Last year my firm exceeded $1 million in revenue.

I've found my passion, I'm actually fulfilling it and it's providing me with a stimulating and rewarding lifestyle.

willing to promote your CLNC® services. That's another thing I learned from Vickie.

My number one rule for securing repeat business is being open to and listening for the attorney's need in each case I accept. Attorney-specific, case-specific is my motto!

For the next three years, I continued to work as a director of nursing services in another skilled nursing facility and ran my part-time CLNC® business from home. Sometimes it was a family affair, with my children working for me. All three of them have filed and scanned medical records. I tried to instill the entrepreneurial spirit and some business savvy as well. During this time, in addition to performing the same services I started with, I added attending mediation conferences, assisting the attorney in preparing MD and nurse testifying experts, and participating in risk management seminars for long term care corporations.

Meeting the Challenges of Growth Brought Me Even Greater Success

While still a part-time CLNC® consultant, I was able to buy a home, eliminate financial dependence on my parents and provide for my three children, including enabling them to participate in sports and many other extracurricular activities they couldn't enjoy previously. During my transition from part time to full time four years ago, my legal nurse consulting revenues were $85,000.

When I reached my goal of quitting the SNF and becoming a full-time Certified Legal Nurse

Today I can do the things I only dreamed of doing when I retire.

Vickie Milazzo Institute provides all the tools you need to get started. Vickie shows you how to make your CLNC® business fun and rewarding.

Consultant^CM, I held a wine and cheese open house to celebrate the opening of my new office and to share my success with friends, family and current and potential attorney-clients. About six months after I went full time, I took Vickie's advice and added my first employee, who's still with me. I also subcontracted with four CLNC® consultants. That year I massively exceeded my goal of grossing $200,000.

Two short years later, my business had expanded by adding more office space, two employees and another CLNC® subcontractor. As a result, my firm doubled its revenues.

As the business continued to grow, I refined our services and added more qualified, high-caliber individuals. I now have a 3,200-square-foot office and a total of ten employees – four nurses plus support and administrative staff. Having the in-house expertise of Certified Legal Nurse Consultants^CM who share my vision is truly exciting.

Business keeps rolling in because we deliver a superior work product to our clients. This generates a prompt response from the attorney: Suzanne, this is awesome. We can do big things with this. Last year my firm exceeded $1 million in revenue.

Today I Can *Do* Things I Only Dreamed of Doing When I Retire

While this kind of financial success is not necessarily the primary goal, it's exciting that I've found my passion, I'm actually fulfilling it and it's providing me with a stimulating and rewarding lifestyle. My eldest is going to college next year. I'm prepared for that expensive college tuition and I never thought I would be.

Balancing the business and my family is still a challenge. At least financially I have the freedom to spend more time with them, knowing and feeling comfortable that someone's still running the office, especially if I want to take off in the middle of the week. Today I can *do* the things I only dreamed of doing when I retire.

I have always had a deep faith in God and commitment to prayer. The Lord has blessed me with the ability to discern what is important in my life and has given me the strength to work hard and learn all I can.

Professionally, I wouldn't be where I am today without becoming a Certified Legal Nurse Consultant^{CM}. There's no other program out there like Vickie's. There is simply no competition. She and Vickie Milazzo Institute provide all the tools you need to get started. She shows you how to make your CLNC® business fun and rewarding, not only financially but in other ways. Being a CLNC® consultant represents a high level of professionalism. The *National Alliance of Certified Legal Nurse Consultants*® embraces networking instead of competition between nurses. I've seen this industry grow and I think it will continue to grow. It's up to CLNC® business owners to uplift the nursing profession and maintain that positive attitude, knowing that there's enough work out there for all of us.

Vickie walks the walk. She's an inspiration, not only as a nurse who pioneered a new industry but also as a keen-minded business-woman who openly shares her secrets.

I come to the *NACLNC*® Conferences for my annual boost. It's my yearly reminder of the power of nurses and the power of nursing in the community. I also get to see Vickie, take part in some fascinating sessions and network with more than 1,200 nurses.

If I could say one thing to my RN peers, I'd advise them to take their fear and do something with it. Evaluate what you want for your life, embrace the fear and then go for it. The next step is following a marketing plan to make sure the business is growing, new cases are coming in and new prospects are hearing about you. You can never take your current clients for granted. Customer service has to be number one. Every single member of my team knows the importance of that. We're human; we make little mistakes. But if you're always there for your attorney-clients, always answering questions, meeting deadlines and following up, those minor human errors will be no biggie.

The CLNC® Mentoring Program is absolutely crucial to your growth into a mature CLNC® consultant. Vickie and her staff are always there for you. No other program is actually there to lift you up when you're down, to provide the support that is so necessary to becoming successful.

Vickie Is My Inspiration as a Successful, Savvy Entrepreneur

Vickie walks the walk. She's an inspiration, not only as a nurse who pioneered a new industry but also as a keen-minded, successful businesswoman who openly shares her secrets. Vickie's wisdom and her generosity with that wisdom have made me stronger, more passionate and driven to succeed for my family and my personal growth.

Vickie lives her motto, "Revolutionizing Nursing Careers One RN at a Time." I'm a categorical example of one of those careers she revolutionized, to the tune of a million-dollar business. What stuck with me the most was her statement that you are a nurse and you can do anything. I truly took that motto to heart.

I always remember where I came from and that I started my CLNC® business from my bedroom. Rebounding from divorce, depression and financial inadequacy was tough, but I have grown tremendously as a person. Today I'm very appreciative that I don't have to work in my bedroom anymore. I love my life. I love my career. I spend time with my children. I consistently bring in a comfortable six-figure income and it just keeps getting better.

Thank you, Vickie, for giving me the motivation and education to become a CLNC® success.

> *I love my career. I spend time with my children. I consistently bring in a comfortable six-figure income and it just keeps getting better.*

I have built a potential $500,000-600,000 a year legal nurse consulting business.

I mailed out 25 packets. Within three days, an attorney at the biggest law firm in my county called me to meet with him.

I Created a Potential Half-Million-Dollar-a-Year CLNC® Business Through My Belief and Vickie's Preparation

by Carmen Stine, RN, BSN, CCM, CLP, CLNC, Delaware

I have been an RN for well over 35 years and became a Certified Legal Nurse Consultant^CM last year. I now have my own very successful CLNC® business.

I learned about legal nurse consulting by seeing Vickie Milazzo Institute ads for 15 years. During that time, I thought of becoming a Certified Legal Nurse Consultant^CM but the timing was never right for one reason or another. Early in my career I felt I wasn't experienced enough and midway through my career, life was happening with family and financial responsibilities. Last year, I saw the ad with Vickie's photo once again and something just clicked inside me. Instinctively, I knew this was my next career move. Having worked in the home healthcare field for seven years, I loved the autonomy, the field work and the attachment to my patients and their families. However, I was getting quite tired of the constant bureaucratic demands. I was at the brink of burnout so the timing for me to pursue a career change was right. I quickly enrolled in the VIP CLNC® Success System with financing.

I watched the CLNC® Certification Program for a total of 65 hours and soon scheduled my CLNC® Certification Exam. Throughout the process of my newfound education, I was excited at the prospect of using my extensive nursing knowledge and experience, creating a business of my own, educating attorneys and others on medical issues (I love to teach) and continuing to help people.

I took the CLNC® Certification Exam, and I was so happy when the screen on the computer displayed my passing score that I cried for about ten minutes. I was now a Certified Legal Nurse Consultant^{CM}. I went home, immediately put all my marketing materials together and mailed out 25 packets. Within three days, an attorney at the biggest law firm in my county called me to meet with him and his paralegal.

He was very excited that I was so close. This firm does only personal injury and medical-malpractice cases. A few days later, I went to my first attorney meeting to sell my CLNC® services. Unbeknownst to me, there were nine attorneys, three paralegals and three executive assistants waiting for me at this meeting. If this was a test for how I would do under pressure, I am proud to say I passed with flying colors.

During my interview, I focused on them and how I could help solve their problems (just like Vickie teaches). I asked several questions about what their biggest challenges were and how they were currently dealing with those challenges. I then explained how my CLNC® services would enhance

During my interview, I focused on them and how I could help solve their problems (just like Vickie teaches).

what they were already doing because I had the benefit of knowing the ins and outs of the hospital structure, workflows, hierarchy, etc. I emphasized that I have always analyzed, assessed, evaluated and made critical decisions about nursing and medical care. I addressed each of their challenges with confirmation that "this is why you need me" (sound familiar?). I emphasized the unique involvement of the paralegals and executive assistants and shared how I could help free them to focus on their respective duties. After 45 minutes, I walked out of the office with nine cases to review. I worked on the three most urgent cases first and returned them within five days. My attorney-clients were very impressed at my timeliness, professionalism, ability to work with their staff and the quality of the reports I provided. I completed the other six reviews within seven business days and again they were very impressed. After the initial reviews, I helped prepare those nine cases for litigation and acquired new cases as well.

Incredibly in the first two cases, I discovered tampering of the medical records. The two attorneys working these cases were awed at my discovery. Both cases settled for significantly more than was previously anticipated. The ability to detect medical tampering has catapulted me to success with this law firm.

I was not at all afraid to put myself out there because I felt so confident with my clinical background, my experience and the education I received from Vickie in the CLNC® Certification

Program. Having prepared myself to market also helped me feel confident.

I think preparation is key to anyone's success. I know in my soul that I have a lot to offer any attorney who is willing to work with me, and with that mindset, I can't fail. My standard of excellence gives me great confidence as well. You have to believe in yourself and what you are offering in order for others to believe in you too. Being focused, self-directed and clear in what you want to accomplish is absolutely crucial for success.

Transitioning from my full-time home healthcare job, where I was earning $120,000/yr to full-time CLNC® consultant at $225/hr took me exactly four weeks. I consult with 12 attorneys in this firm, billing $8,000-10,000 a week on average. I have built a potential $500,000-600,000 a year legal nurse consulting business in the last six months. My goal is to create a $1 million business within the next two years.

My life has changed forever, in more ways than I can include here. These are just some of the highlights:

- ▶ I work from home: no commute, no traffic, no weather issues, no burnout!
- ▶ I built a brand-new 10,000 sq. ft. home.
- ▶ I created my own financial freedom.
- ▶ I built a successful CLNC® business with a high profile in the legal community.
- ▶ I gained an abundance of new friends and business associates.

I discovered tampering of the records. The two attorneys working these cases were awed at my discovery.

My life has changed forever. I built a brand-new 10,000 sq. ft. home.

I work from home: no commute, no traffic, no weather issues, no burnout!

Of course, no success is possible without a support system. First and foremost, I thank God every day for my blessings. Many thanks to my husband and my mother for their endless support. Equal appreciation to Vickie for the amazing preparation I have been so privileged to obtain. As Vickie says: "*We are nurses and we can do anything!®*"

In My 4th Month I Billed $16,000 and Became a Full-Time CLNC® Consultant

by Becky Mungai, RN, BA, CLNC, Florida

> **"** *Soon I was billing so many hours as a CLNC® consultant — $16,000 in my fourth month alone! — that I could no longer work at the hospital.* **"**

I am thrilled to have the opportunity to share the success of my CLNC® career. I could tell my story a million times because it's so exciting to have finally achieved all of my professional goals. I grew up with the aspiration of becoming an obstetrician. I entered college as a pre-med student and it wasn't long before I realized how challenging being a doctor and a hands-on parent would be.

I wanted to be a mom more than anything. I decided to change direction towards my other interests, teaching and psychology. I got a B.A. in psychology, a minor in coaching and completed all my teaching courses but quit during student teaching. I didn't love it. I couldn't deny that I loved medicine, so I became a nurse.

I'm 47 now, and I've felt like I shortchanged myself my entire life and hadn't reached my full potential. I wanted to achieve a certain status and financial level, and I never got that from nursing. As an ED nurse, I had a tremendous amount of responsibility and yet I was treated as insignificant compared to the physicians. I graduated at the top of my high school class and received a full college scholarship with early entrance and honors on admission. I graduated summa cum laude with two degrees and my teaching coursework completed. It was always frustrating to have so much education, so little respect and such minimal compensation. I was sick of it.

Vickie's Big Smile Beckoned Me to Escape a "Toxic" ED Environment

I decided to make a change. In Oregon, I had an awesome job working dayshift and basically running my own cosmetic laser business with a talented and well-respected plastic surgeon who compensated me well, gave me autonomy and respected my intellect. And while I appreciated this opportunity, it still didn't meet my list of criteria for success. I soon grew bored and the sunshine and water were calling me, so we put two kids in college, took our little one and moved to Florida. We bought a big, beautiful house on the water with a huge mortgage (actually a moderate mortgage but adding hurricane insurance made it huge). My husband, following his heart and desire to find his passion, left a successful corporate-America career and started a video production company.

I expected my nursing salary in Florida to be about the same as Oregon, but it was only half as much. The panhandle of Florida offered sunshine and white sand beaches but the unique situation I had in Oregon was not available. I went back to the Peds ED. I love kids and emergency care but in addition to the low pay, I was dismayed by the sketchy quality of medical care. I was not proud to

I wanted to achieve a certain status and financial level, and I never got that from nursing. I was sick of it.

As a side benefit I even lost 25 pounds when I started my CLNC® business. It was effortless because I'm so happy.

be part of that ED. The other nurses felt the same way and their response was to constantly complain and create a "toxic" environment. It was sucking the life out of me.

I needed to get out of that situation, and I felt like this was my last chance to make a change. I had always been interested in law and started searching for a law program. But I had a ten-year old, and if I went to law school, I'd still have to work full-time and I'd shortchange him. I just wasn't willing to make that sacrifice. My list of criteria became: to be appropriately compensated for my knowledge and work ethic; to work from home (my office looks out onto the bay with dolphins swimming by); to never work another holiday or weekend; to have the freedom to care for my child when he is sick; to go on field trips; to volunteer in the classroom; and to be respected and commended for my expertise.

For years I'd seen Vickie's smiling picture in the ads for her CLNC® Certification Program. I saw her program as the perfect combination of my two interests; law and medicine. When I realized how comprehensive her training was, I ordered everything she offered. It was my belief that if one nurse could do this, I could! And if I was going to invest in myself, I was going all the way. I was setting myself up for success. I ordered the VIP CLNC® Success System.

Before I went to the CLNC® Certification Seminar, I studied the CLNC® Certification Program and the *Core Curriculum for Legal Nurse Consulting*® textbook. I did this for two reasons: To decrease my

> *Every day is spent doing exactly what I want to be doing. I finally feel like I'm getting the professional respect I've sought my entire life.*

test-taking anxiety and to get the most out of the week-long seminar. I know that anxiety makes it difficult to absorb information and like I said, I was setting myself up for success. I had all the information – now I wanted to solidify it and grab all the nuances that would be offered at Vickie's seminar.

By the time I walked into the CLNC® Certification Seminar, I was already prepared to take the CLNC® Certification Exam. I used those days – plus the *NACLNC*® Apprenticeship – to fine tune.

As a side benefit I even lost 25 pounds when I started my CLNC® business. It was effortless and I think it was because I'm so happy.

Every day is spent doing exactly what I want to be doing. I finally feel like I'm getting the professional respect I've sought my entire life. I'm not only being treated like an equal, I'm being treated as a tremendous asset. The attorneys need me and they respect my intelligence. They pump me up constantly. Gone are the days of the "toxic" hospital environment.

Between the attorneys and Vickie Milazzo Institute, I am ecstatic! Vickie gives you all the tools you need, and the Institute holds your hand every step of the way. When something great happens, they're there to cheer you on, as if they are family. That's unheard of, especially in nursing.

As a Certified Legal Nurse Consultant℠, I finally feel like I've arrived.

I Branded My CLNC® Business Like Vickie Taught and Networked My Way to Success

The first thing I did was put together a promotional packet along with my resume and a list of my CLNC® services.

For 23 years I had worked in pediatric emergency and attended over 2,000 deliveries as the primary neonatal nurse. I'm confident of my knowledge in these areas. In addition, I found that my specialties, birth trauma and pediatric emergency trauma, are highly litigious. So I did an Internet search on birth trauma attorneys. I'd read an attorney's bio and if I had something in common with him, I'd call. If an attorney played college basketball, went to Phillips Academy, was a Theta or went to Whitman College, I'd call them. I used that connection to get past the gatekeeper.

The first time I tried this I called the attorney's office and said, "Hi, this is Becky Mungai. Is Kirby in? We went to Whitman College together." The secretary didn't ask any questions. She just put me through. That attorney's partner became my first case.

While Christmas shopping I got a call from an attorney who said, "Kirby gave me your number. I need you and another L&D nurse to look at a case and give me a verbal opinion." All it took was that one attorney's call to fuel my energy for my CLNC® business. I had my first case and my first subcontracting opportunity.

I recently returned from a legal conference in Nevada. I came home with seven new attorney-clients and 11 cases.

I currently work with attorneys in 19 states. I'm on track to achieve six figures!

I Billed $16,000 in My Fourth Month

The day I came back from the CLNC® 6-Day Certification Seminar, I went half time at the hospital. I was determined to invest time in my CLNC® business. I couldn't work full time and start my business or someone would be shortchanged, and it wasn't going to be my child.

Soon I was billing so many hours as a CLNC® consultant – $16,000 in my fourth month alone! – that I could no longer work at the hospital.

I recently returned from a legal conference in Nevada. It was my sixth conference this year. I came home with seven new attorney-clients and 11 cases. In addition, I currently have several cases in progress and work with attorneys in 19 states. I'm scheduled for three more conferences in the next few months and have been asked to present at a legal seminar. I'm on track to achieve six figures!

With each new case, I learn more about managing a successful CLNC® business. In one early case, I was talking to the attorney and he mentioned that he already had his team in place and didn't need anyone else. Nevertheless, the attorney went on to describe a case over the phone. I gave him some questions to ask his expert and the defendant. When I followed up to see how it went he said he had forgotten to ask some of the questions. He responded with, "Why don't I send you some of the records to see what you think. Just put me on the clock." What he sent was 18 pages. For a couple of weeks, I couldn't think of a single thing I hadn't

If you have a choice you'd choose the best, and that's what Vickie provides. I absolutely recommend the VIP CLNC® Success System.

The unlimited mentoring with the CLNC® Mentors is phenomenal.

already told him. But he'd said to put him on the clock, and I was determined to find something! Finally, I decided to put what I had already told him in chronology format to see if anything else popped out at me. Sure enough, I discovered a tampering issue. The attorney was so busy, he didn't comment – but more than a month later he called and said, "That tampering issue you found blew this case wide open. All of a sudden we have additional discovery. Thank you so much!"

I Love Making Connections and They Always Pay Off

I love connecting with new attorneys. It's my favorite part of this business. I met with one attorney who's very well respected in town. She has her own nurse consultant working in-house, but she agreed to meet with me anyway. I asked her why, and she said, "I just like how you sound on the phone." As a result of meeting her, she has referred two attorneys to me and I've done a lot of work with one of them. She had a tough case several months ago and emailed me for emotional support. Our relationship continues to grow.

I was recently requested to fly to Houston to teach an attorney about newborn resuscitation for one of her cases. She was flying in from the West Coast. We met with another attorney I do cases for and her partner who is an anesthesiologist. We spent a couple days teaching, working up the case and brainstorming some of my other cases. She is one of my favorite attorney-clients.

The CLNC® Mentors give great advice and always lead me in the right direction. It's the support network I had been looking for in nursing and had yet to find.

The VIP CLNC® Success System Is the Nordstrom of Legal Nurse Consulting

The first thing I received from the Institute was the free CLNC® Success Stories book. I also watched the legal nurse consulting video and I read the Success Stories book. Then when I'd go for a walk, I'd create my CLNC® Success Story in my head. I believe that if you think you'll be successful, you will. Vickie teaches the same thing. When she says, "We are successful CLNC® consultants," she's putting that in our heads – dress for success, act successful and you'll be successful. It'll all happen – and it did.

If you have a choice of going to the best four-year college to prepare for your career, would you take a correspondence course instead? No, you'd choose the best, and that's what Vickie provides. I absolutely recommend the VIP CLNC® Success System. The added cost of the VIP CLNC® Success System, when you divide it out over five years, comes down to pennies basically, but you're investing in yourself by getting it all. As a VIP you also feel more successful while you're in the program.

The unlimited mentoring with the CLNC® Mentors is phenomenal. I tend to hold onto a problem too long – I want to solve it myself and then I panic because I need the answer right this second. The CLNC® Mentors get right back to me. They support me all the way. They never act like I'm taking up their time. They want to know,

"Have I answered all your questions? Do you need anything else?" I feel like they "have my back." They want me to succeed. There is no competition. It's all about complementing my efforts and pumping me up. The CLNC® Mentors give great advice and always lead me in the right direction. It's the support network I had been looking for in nursing and had yet to find.

Vickie gives you all the tools. She's dotted every "i" and crossed every "t." She could not do it better than she has. She's right up there with Nordstrom. I went to college with one of the Nordstroms, and that's who Vickie is. Someone could take what she has done with this business and use it as a business model at Harvard. Nothing is missing. She has everything down, from branding your business to supporting you while you learn and not dropping the ball afterwards. I've reached my professional goal as a CLNC® consultant.

I have gone from reviewing cases to traveling with attorneys across the country, Canada, Mexico and Panama attending depositions, mediations, trials, medical-malpractice conferences, legal seminars and soon to be speaking at my first legal convention.

I hold phone consults on the white sand beaches of Pensacola while watching my son surf. Two days ago, I noticed the bay water in my "backyard" to be perfect glass. I took a break from my cases and went knee boarding with my 11-year-old and his friends. Twelve dolphins joined us and it was one of the best days ever.

> *Becoming a CLNC® consultant has offered me the flexibility to catch the joys of life. Not only am I finally making the money I deserve, my life is everything I've dreamed it to be.*

*I have
exceeded
my income
goals each
year –
making
four times
what
I would
have as a
full-time
nurse.*

Becoming a CLNC® consultant has offered me the flexibility to catch the joys of life. Not only am I finally making the money I deserve, my life is everything I've dreamed it to be. I have complete independence and freedom to work when and with whom I wish. Life is amazing! In times of economic uncertainty I have exceeded my income goals each and every year – making four times what I would have as a full-time staff nurse. I am truly blessed and look forward to another fantastic year.

Ugly Duckling to Golden Goose — How I Conquered My Fear

by Lawrence H. Frace, RN, CLNC, New Jersey

Two years ago I was a registered nurse with 26 years of experience. I liked my job as a night tour nursing supervisor, but I was suffering from what I call "professional bradycardia." After taking Vickie's CLNC® Certification Seminar, I immediately knew my professional (and personal) life was about to change.

I had tried other part-time activities in addition to my full-time nursing career. I was a licensed real estate salesperson, a soil and site evaluator, an Amway distributor, a part-time farmer growing sweet corn on my dad's farm. I even sent away for a program on how to buy real estate with little or no money down. But I finally found my niche as a CLNC® consultant.

Fear Was My Stumbling Block

However, as a new Certified Legal Nurse Consultant℠ I faced a huge stumbling block that initially held me back. I'm sharing my experience so that maybe the obstacle I tripped over time and time again will not be a stumbling block for others. That stumbling block was fear, pure unadulterated fear.

> *After taking Vickie's CLNC® Certification Seminar, I immediately knew my professional (and personal) life was about to change.*

> *I finally found my niche as a Certified Legal Nurse Consultant℠.*

I am 6-foot 2-inches tall, two hundred and some-odd pounds, and for the first time I found myself confronting professional fear. So I did what any reasonable and prudent new Certified Legal Nurse Consultant[CM] would do. I procrastinated!

Oh, I dove right in from day one, setting up my office in my basement, complete with used office furniture, fax machine and multiple phone lines, including an 800 number. I went out and purchased a brand new computer and one of those dot-com address things and posted my website on the Internet, SpectrumMedicalLegal.com. Boy, was I proud of that!

I went through Vickie's *Core Curriculum for Legal Nurse Consulting*® textbook again and again, 30 minutes each day. I subscribed to a host of nursing journals. I started compiling an electronic medical-legal library that I thought was second to none. I went to libraries and book sales and purchased used medical and legal textbooks, carefully displaying them on the walls in my new basement office.

I also created a letter agreement, just like the sample in the *Core Curriculum*, to use for all my anticipated cases. But you know what? I didn't send any of my promotional packets out to attorneys.

Six months later, I said to myself, "But wait a minute. I still have no cases. What's wrong with this picture?" Then it dawned on me: It was fear…fear of actually getting that first case.

> *I sent out seven marketing packets. Two law firms called, and they both wanted to meet with me.*

I Tried Marketing with My Fingers Crossed

I put my foot down. I finally sent out seven – count them seven – marketing packets. You'll never guess what happened. Two law firms called, and they both wanted to meet with me. Now I thought to myself, "I am in *big* trouble."

I met with attorney #1, and he told me all the real work on the case was done; it just needed to be tabbed and paginated. I walked away from that one and said, "Thank God, at least I didn't get an actual case to work on."

Attorney #2 had told me on the phone that her case involved a person with a physical disability being treated unfairly by an employer. I set up a date to meet with attorney #2 and did what any novice CLNC® consultant would do prior to that all-important first meeting. I researched the disability and how it could be accommodated in the workplace according to cutting-edge, authoritative reports in journals and textbooks. I placed this information in my briefcase and gave it to attorney #2 when I met her.

She looked through the information and said, "Thank you, this is just what I needed." Then she shook my hand, and that was the end of the meeting.

Now I remember Vickie saying, "Give attorneys what they want and one thing more." The problem was, how did I know, novice that I was, that I'd handed the attorney that "one thing more" up front and thus got no compensation on that case?

I met with that attorney, and he gave me the case, the chart, the 'whole enchilada.' I left with both chart and check in hand.

Writing the report was fun, which surprised me since I thought that would be one of the most difficult tasks.

I chalked my loss up to experience and said once again, "Thank God, at least I didn't get an actual case to work on." I left attorney #2's office empty-handed.

Still having no cases under my CLNC® belt, I started marketing a product to attorneys across the nation, an idea I had gleaned from Vickie. Several weeks later I started receiving checks in the mail. This was great – go to the mailbox, get the money, send out the product. But now I felt guilty. Here I was, marketing a product to attorneys, and I still did not have a case.

Then I Tried Marketing for Real

I put my foot down again – this time really hard – and sent out seven more marketing packets. Wouldn't you know it, one of the law firms called me. I met with that attorney, and he gave me the case, the chart, the "whole enchilada."

By the way, here's a tip on getting paid by attorneys: Get your money up front. That's Vickie's tip not mine, and it works. When that first attorney-client asked about my fee, I told him what I charged and stated that I get my fee up front. He looked at me, paused, then opened his checkbook and wrote me a check. I left with both chart and check in hand.

Then fear turned into panic as I thought, "Now what am I going to do?" Delving into the chart at home, I created a chronology, got a real feel for the case, took notes and put into practice what I'd learned from Vickie nearly a year-and-a-half earlier. And guess what? Writing the report was fun, which surprised me since I had always thought that would be one of the most difficult tasks.

A month later when I handed the attorney his report, I did include that "one thing more." But this time I got it right, and he was pleased. In fact, he gave me case #2, and without my asking, out came his checkbook. "I know, Larry," he said, "you get your money up front."

"Wow, I trained that attorney well," I thought as I left his office with chart and check in hand. Since then, he has given me case #3 and, yes, his checkbook automatically opened up before I left his office.

Your Nursing Skills and Credentials Are for Real

As nurses we often underestimate our abilities, especially if we're doing something new to us, like legal nurse consulting. Don't under-estimate your abilities as I did. With your nursing training and experience, coupled with Vickie's knowledge, guidance and CLNC® resources, believe me, you will succeed.

Imagine getting paid for work you absolutely love to do. It's almost like stealing – well, almost. All of Vickie's Certified Legal Nurse Consultants^{CM} have a powerful, marketable product to offer. We all have our CLNC® Certification. Don't ever forget that.

> *All of Vickie's Certified Legal Nurse Consultants*^{CM} *have a powerful, marketable product – our CLNC® Certification.*

Remember the saying, "You have nothing to fear but fear itself." It took me one-and-a-half years to realize that concept. Don't let that happen to you. Just go out there and "Do It." Do your best and follow Vickie's plan.

Vickie Is for Real

I will close with this true story about Vickie herself. I know it's true because I was there. On the last day of our CLNC® Certification Seminar, our group circulated and signed a thank-you card that read something like this:

> *Dear Vickie, you took all of us Ugly Ducklings
> and turned us into Golden Geese.*

One student surprised Vickie by presenting the card to her on stage. As Vickie began to read the card, her eyes welled up and for several moments she could not speak. When she did speak, her voice began to quiver – she was visibly moved by that simple card. That's when I knew Vickie truly cares about all her Ducklings and Golden Geese.

Thank you, Vickie, and your fine organization for "awakening my potential and the nurse within me." And thank you, Vickie, for being you.

My CLNC® Success Includes the Freedom to Walk Away at 3:30pm

by Bobbi Black, RN, CLNC, Iowa

After working in a large clinic for 22 years, I retired. I was 48, my life was changing, my workplace was changing and I qualified for early retirement, so I took it. My family was growing up, and I began to wonder, "What am I going to do now?" Then I found Vickie Milazzo Institute's LegalNurse. com website and became intrigued. I knew I had the experience as a nurse to become a Certified Legal Nurse Consultant^CM – I decided to take the CLNC® Certification Seminar. Vickie's CLNC® Certification Program is the key to my CLNC® success.

Becoming a Certified Legal Nurse Consultant^CM has such a positive impact on my life. It spells *freedom* – more financial freedom, being able to work from home doing what I love to do any time I want, but also being able to walk away from it at 3:30 in the afternoon. I'm free to walk downstairs to find my husband in his office – he also works from home. (Separate offices work best for us during the day because of business phone calls and other distractions.) We are then free to choose what we want to do with the rest of our day.

When asked by other nurses if a career in legal nurse consulting can be successful, I repeat what

I'm living my dream of being a successful CLNC® consultant, having a great time and being rewarded financially for the work I do!

Vickie told me, "Absolutely, if you're passionate about it."

Market, market, market, even when you're busy. Anywhere I market my CLNC® business, I show up with independence and confidence, just like Vickie taught me. I walk in the door and say, "Here I am. I can help you."

My CLNC® business really took off when I located a group of attorneys and camped out on their door step. Today those attorneys are some of my best clients. One of the attorneys recently told me, "The reason I hired you is because I was tired of stepping over you when I came through the door in the morning." We laugh about it now, but my persistence paid off.

In Vickie's CLNC® Certification Program, she encourages her students to send out a newsletter to attorney-prospects and clients. My newsletter helps me connect with attorneys and I can count on receiving numerous phone calls each time I send one.

My CLNC® consulting work is always interesting. Many RNs think legal nurse consultants consult only on medical malpractice or personal injury cases. Some of my favorite cases are the ones that I wouldn't think I'd be involved in, like a murder trial or a legal malpractice case involving a will.

The case outcomes can also be very exciting. My first big attorney-client asked me to review a medical malpractice case for merit. I found a gross

*Becoming a Certified Legal Nurse Consultant*CM *has such a positive impact on my life. It spells* freedom.

My nursing experience and Vickie's CLNC® Certification Program were the biggest factors in winning the case.

deviation in the standards of care and located an expert for the attorney. That case went to mediation and settled for a larger amount than anyone expected.

While that litigation was in progress, my attorney-client asked me to begin work on another case. A doctor had previously reviewed the case's medical records, but when the attorney asked for my help, I discovered numerous things the doctor had overlooked. Then, right before the case went to trial, the attorney asked me to accompany him to court. When the defense expert denied the validity of a particular radiology report, I whispered to my attorney-client, "Trust me on this – show him *this* report." The second report invalidated the medical expert for the defense and upended their case. My nursing experience and Vickie's CLNC® Certification Program were the biggest factors in winning the case.

A large part of my CLNC® consulting success is due to Vickie's enthusiasm and her encouraging words, such as We Are Nurses and We Can Do Anything!®

Vickie's CLNC® Mentoring Program is another part of my CLNC® consulting success. I enjoy working through the problems I encounter. I contact the CLNC® Mentors any time I'm stymied. It's reassuring to brainstorm with these CLNC® Pros.

What makes my CLNC® business successful? By thinking outside the box, using my nursing

Vickie's CLNC® Mentoring Program is part of my CLNC® consulting success. It's reassuring to brainstorm with these CLNC® Pros.

*Anywhere
I market
my CLNC®
business,
I show
up with
independence
and
confidence,
just like
Vickie
taught me.*

skills and remembering Vickie's CLNC® training, I successfully evaluate cases and help my attorney-clients gain the best outcomes. I'm so excited about my CLNC® career. I'm living my dream of being a successful CLNC® consultant, having a great time and being rewarded financially for the work I do!

Shocked to Success with Vital Signs Still Intact

by Arlene Santiago-Tribbett, RN, BSN, CLNC, New Jersey

For the past eight years, I've been a home care and ED/trauma nurse. My nursing career had become unsatisfying, so I began searching in a new career direction. I thought about graduate school, but none of the programs seemed worthy of my time or money. Before becoming a nurse, I was a police officer, and the law always fascinated me. So when I saw an ad for Vickie's CLNC® Certification Program in a nursing magazine, I researched the field and signed up for the Institute's program.

The CLNC® Certification Seminar impressed me from the first day. Vickie gave away information so freely, and I experienced nurses from all over the country coming together in unity and fully supportive of each other. The seminar was so motivating that I regained the pride I once had for nursing. Vickie and her CLNC® Certification Program did that for me.

The week after the seminar was like a dream. I had an appointment to see an attorney for personal reasons. I told him I was a Certified Legal Nurse Consultant^CM and mentioned the services I provided. He stopped me in mid-sentence and called his associates into his office to hear what I had to say. "Where have you been?" he asked

Vickie gave away information so freely. The seminar was so motivating that I regained the pride I once had for nursing.

That one week with Vickie was the most challenging, yet the most exciting of my life.

and explained that his firm desperately needed a qualified CLNC® consultant.

I told him I charged $125/hr and needed a 50% retainer, and he gave me three cases with the promise of two more. He went on to say that he would introduce me to other attorneys who could use my CLNC® services.

I am still in shock. I never expected any of this. That one week with Vickie was the most challenging, yet the most exciting of my life. Now, I actually have work in my hands. My life is headed in a new, exciting and profitable direction I could never have imagined before I attended Vickie's CLNC® Certification Seminar.

My life is headed in a new, exciting and profitable direction I could never have imagined before I attended Vickie's CLNC® Certification Seminar.

Vickie's CLNC® Certification Gives Hope and Confidence

by Heidi Santiago, RN, CLNC, New York

S o many of the seminars that I have been to as a nurse have not lived up to what they say. Vickie's CLNC® Certification Seminar certainly proved to be different for me.

I drove home from the seminar to my son's football game that night and immediately applied Vickie's 3-foot rule.

I started talking to the gentleman next to me whose son was also in the game. When I mentioned that I just returned home from a seminar, he asked, "What kind of seminar?" I replied, "Legal nurse consulting." We began to talk. He said he was a medical malpractice attorney from a large firm and that he had a case he wanted me to review. He also said he had heard about Vickie and the Institute.

That same weekend at a wine and cheese party, my brother introduced me to a personal injury attorney. When I asked him to get me into his firm to meet the other attorneys, he said, "Sure." I networked just like Vickie taught us, and in only one weekend I got one case and an introduction that will put me in touch with other potential attorney-clients.

The most beneficial part of Vickie's CLNC® Certification Seminar was the amount of confidence that she imparted to us all. Now I can walk into any attorney's office with the confidence of success,

> *Vickie's program taught me how to succeed in a business that has already started to provide an exceptional living for me and my family.*

> *A medical malpractice attorney had a case he wanted me to review. He had heard about Vickie and the Institute.*

*Vickie
taught us
to never
devalue
our nursing
knowledge
but to put
a top-dollar
price on it.*

knowing legal terminology, knowing the services I can provide and knowing that attorneys will pay for my nursing knowledge and experience.

I walked away from Vickie's CLNC® Certification Seminar with hope. Vickie taught us to never devalue our nursing knowledge but to put a top-dollar price on it. I thought I was crazy to start my own business now, at age 40 with 12 years in home health nursing. I've tried so many home-based businesses from network marketing to mail order, that never ever panned out. Vickie's program taught me how to succeed in a business that has already started to provide an exceptional living for me and my family.

How I Knew It Was Time to Cut the Cord from My RN Job

by Susan Schaab,
RN, BSN, CLNC, Montana

After I became a Certified Legal Nurse Consultant^CM I built my attorney-client base from one to four attorney-clients while still working at the hospital. Many weeks I worked 10-15 hours of overtime at my RN job in the ambulatory surgery department. And while this added to my checking account, I felt physically drained, mentally bored and definitely not in control of my nursing career. My CLNC® business suffered because my hospital job took priority.

Some days I would come home exhausted and then receive a call from an attorney-client. I was instantly energized and my mind was sharp and clear. That's when I realized I had found my passion as a Certified Legal Nurse Consultant^CM. I also realized that the all-consuming hospital was a threat to my passion and I had to develop a concrete plan – a way out for good.

I created a chart comparing my hourly wage as an RN to my hourly fee as a Certified Legal Nurse Consultant^CM. Looking at that chart mentally set me free. I saw that I could replace my 40 hours per week pay with just 10 hours per week as a CLNC® consultant. It suddenly became doable and not

I could replace my 40 hours per week pay with just 10 hours per week as a CLNC® consultant.

Marketing became almost effortless through referrals.

just some long sought-after dream. I then created a calendar which highlighted all my days off and I realized how much time I had to build my CLNC® business. I set weekly and monthly goals for actual hours billed and put all my extra time and energy into achieving those goals. Some weeks and months I would meet or exceed them; other months I would fall behind, but my overall trend was positive in building my CLNC® business.

I focused on marketing to my current attorney-clients after listening to the CLNC® marketing audio programs. I kept in touch by delivering treats to the offices on atypical holidays like St. Patrick's Day and Halloween. This not only reminded the attorneys about me, but also endeared me to the support staff. Gatekeepers became friends and supporters instead of roadblocks. As my cases concluded and had positive outcomes for my attorney-clients, my reputation was established and marketing became almost effortless through referrals. Eventually my attorney-client list expanded from my small town to cities across the state.

Although my CLNC® business income was consistent, leaving the security of the hospital was still frightening. Getting a paycheck every two weeks is very reassuring and comforting. Again, I wrote down exactly what I was earning at the hospital and compared that to my CLNC® earnings. I realized I was actually losing money by working at the hospital. I was billing $125/hr to attorneys, so the $60/hr for overtime shifts was not worth

> *I was actually losing money by working at the hospital.*

> *I was billing $125/hr to attorneys. $60/hr for overtime shifts was not worth the wear and tear on my body.*

the wear and tear on my body. Health insurance was increasing by 15%, yet I would get only a 1% raise, meaning I would be making 14% less than the previous year! Although hospitals are seductive and seem safe and secure, I knew I really had no control in that environment including the risk of RN layoffs.

I dropped to part-time status at my hospital job and put even more effort into marketing to attorney-prospects. My husband was laid off right after this change, but the strength of my CLNC® business soon made up for his lost income. He was able to make a career change and earn less because of my increased income. Six months later I left my hospital job and reached my dream of becoming an independent Certified Legal Nurse Consultant℠!

It pays to know when to cut the cord and put all of your efforts into your CLNC® business.

My husband was laid off but my CLNC® business made up for his lost income.

I left my hospital job and reached my dream.

Take the Fast Track to Financial Freedom

I Am Living My Passion in Tennessee Making $175,000 This Year as a Certified Legal Nurse Consultant^{CM}

by Sheila Silvus Chesanow, RN, MS, CLNC, Tennessee

A fter I became a Certified Legal Nurse Consultant^{CM}, I worked for a corporation doing internal auditing. After two years, a CLNC® friend told me about an opportunity to have an exclusive Certified Legal Nurse Consultant^{CM} contract with an attorney. At first I wasn't sure I wanted an exclusive contract with

> This year I will make about $175,000.

> The benefits of being a Certified Legal Nurse Consultant^{CM} are endless. I enjoy staying at home.

any attorney because I did not know if he would have enough work for me. I was wrong. I ended up signing a contract with this attorney-client for $150,000 annually for 40 hours a week. This year I will make about $175,000.

Technology has been a big plus for my CLNC® business. My husband retired and we moved to Tennessee. My attorney-client lives in California. Technology allows me to work full time at home out of an office that used to be part of our barn as I watch over llamas grazing outside.

One of the best things I've adopted from one of Tom's Tech Tips (from Vickie's Legal Nurse Consulting blog) was dual monitors. I review the files from my attorney-client on one screen while I write my report using the second screen.

I also take my work on the road when I travel. My husband races cars so I can just pack up my bag with my laptop and go with him. It's great because my legal nurse consulting business is completely portable.

The benefits of being a Certified Legal Nurse Consultant[CM] are endless. I work out every morning, have coffee with friends, then I go to work. The more I work, the more money I make. I can work 50 hours one week and take a day off the next whenever I choose. In my prior job, I only slept in my own bed about eight nights a month because I had to travel so much. Now as a Certified Legal Nurse Consultant[CM], I enjoy staying at home here in Tennessee.

"The NACLNC® Directory has a wealth of CLNC® consultants who I can refer business to or recommend as experts."

When I worked at a full-time job, I could count my friends on one hand. Now, I am more involved in my community in Tennessee and I'm active in the charities that are important to me.

I was going to semi-retire, do a little CLNC® work but not really do much. However, I have stayed busy and have had numerous offers for additional legal nurse consulting work. When this happens, I contact my network of CLNC® peers. The *NACLNC*® Directory has a wealth of CLNC® consultants who I can refer business to or recommend as experts.

My advice to nurses is to stop waiting – do it now. Become a Certified Legal Nurse Consultant[CM] today. Stop procrastinating!

My advice to nurses is to stop waiting – do it now.

I Earned $125,000 in 4 Months as a Certified Legal Nurse Consultant^{CM}

by Darlene Bellows, RN, CLNC, Tennessee

I was the director of nursing at a nursing home when I decided to become a Certified Legal Nurse Consultant^{CM}. One day, a staff nurse told me she was taking the CLNC® Certification Program. She shared some of the information with me, and it piqued my interest.

A year later, I left the director of nursing position and accepted a position in the legal department of my long term care company. I began reviewing medical records involved in litigation for the in-house attorney. Then the company hired a new president who began an initiative to reduce the number of lawsuits. He had the foresight to recognize how valuable I could be as a Certified Legal Nurse Consultant^{CM}. The company paid for me to take the CLNC® Certification Seminar in May.

Thrilled and excited, I headed for Orlando to become a Certified Legal Nurse Consultant^{CM}. I never thought I'd make it through that week. There was so much information and so many new things to learn. But with Vickie constantly reminding us that we were successful CLNC® consultants, I passed the test.

I took my new knowledge back to work and continued assisting the company in defending against lawsuits. I was promoted to director of the department, hired another nurse and sent her to the CLNC® Certification Seminar in October.

I Accepted My Husband's Outrageous Holiday Challenge

I soon realized I was doing the job of a legal nurse consultant and getting paid $35/hr instead of the $100-$150/hr I could be making on my own. When I complained about this to my husband, he said, "Why don't you try it part time and see if you like it?"

That was in early December. With the holidays looming, our son's wedding scheduled for two days after Christmas and a houseful of guests expected for both events, I said, "Maybe after the first of the year."

My husband quickly came back with, "What are you waiting for?" I always accept a challenge, especially from my husband. He has steered me in the right direction for the last 20 years.

The next day I called a defense attorney who handled some of my company's cases in Florida. I asked if he thought I could succeed at legal nurse consulting. He said I would be great, and he would keep me busy full time. I told him to send me just one case for now and tell me how I did.

The following week, just days before Christmas (and the wedding), the attorney sent me the

The company president had the foresight to recognize how valuable I could be as a Certified Legal Nurse Consultant℠.

I called a defense attorney. He said I would be great, and he would keep me busy full time.

medical records. Not a large case, but big enough for my first one. He asked if I could report back to him by New Year's Day. Once again I was challenged, and I rose to the occasion and got the assignment done in plenty of time. The feedback I received was that my work was exactly what he needed.

My Part-Time CLNC® Career Blossomed Into Full-Time Success

From that point, I continued to work at my full-time job, then come home every night and worked several hours on my new part-time job, as well as up to ten hours on the weekends. No one at my full-time job knew I was moonlighting, but they wondered why all of a sudden I only worked eight hours instead of my usual 12-14-hour days.

Within three months my legal nurse consulting cases were piling up so much that I had to seek help from a CLNC® subcontractor. I heard another nurse in the office complaining that she could earn much more as a Certified Legal Nurse Consultant^CM and really wanted to pursue it. I recruited her as a subcontractor. Together, we continued turning out the work for another few months.

After attending my first *National Alliance of Certified Legal Nurse Consultants*^CM (*NACLNC®*) Conference in March, I went home and told my husband my goal was to be on my own no later than the end of the year. Two events soon sped up the process. First, my part-time CLNC® career was

> *Within three months my legal nurse consulting cases were piling up so much that I had to seek help from a CLNC® subcontractor.*

generating enough work that I had to hire another subcontractor. My goal was and still is to produce top quality work and get it back to the attorney-client in a timely manner. Second, management changed the direction of our department at my full-time job. This made it easy for me to decide to jump in with both feet and go full time as a CLNC® consultant.

The decision was still scary. All I could think was, "What if I don't get any more cases? Good thing my husband loves peanut-butter-and-jelly sandwiches and I diet most of the time."

Nevertheless, I made the plunge in May. For a short while, I could not keep up with the records. I sent my marketing packet to every defense attorney I had come to know through my former company. I also phoned these attorneys to let them know where I was and what I was doing. As a result, within four months as a full-time independent CLNC® consultant, I billed more than $125,000.

Currently, I consult for four nursing home defense attorneys. They keep my CLNC® business growing. I organize and review medical records; prepare brief or detailed chronologies and narrative summaries; do research and phone consultation; and help long term care companies assess their medical records for liability exposure and documentation accuracy.

One case makes me especially proud – analyzing four years of one patient's nursing home records. The assignment took me 89 hours. When I asked my attorney-client for feedback, he said, "You

He phoned to say my chronology was the best work he had ever seen.

It took me about three months to realize I did not have to feel guilty if I took a day off to pamper myself.

certainly are detailed. I'll call back when I get through it." Two weeks later he phoned to say my chronology was the best work he had ever seen. Everything he needed from the record was in my CLNC® report, and he would be able to use it instead of hauling the volumes of medical records to depositions and mediations. He appreciated how thorough I had been.

Learning to Break the 8-5 Habit Was Part of the Fun

After years of working an 8-5 job, it was hard for me to break the habit. It took me about three months to realize I did not have to feel guilty if I went for a walk with my 84-year-old dad, had lunch with friends, took a day off to pamper myself or spent time with my grandchildren. My best friend and I took our first "girl trip" together to Florida. Of course, I had my laptop, medical records and marketing brochures with me, and I had appointments to see more attorneys.

The money is great. My CLNC® business continues to be very successful. I've had up to 20 cases in progress at one time and as many as five subcontractors working with me. Last year I billed $330,000. But the greatest satisfaction comes when an attorney calls or emails to say, "Your work was awesome. It will be a great help to me in depositions, mediations and at trial."

My success has allowed my husband to retire and help me in my business. In the past couple of years we have taken three fabulous vacations. I've also had time to spend with my three wonderful grandchildren and with other Certified Legal Nurse Consultants^{CM}.

I attribute my CLNC® success to several things: my many years of nursing experience; my experience in the risk management and legal departments in long term care; my supportive family and friends who encouraged me to take a leap of faith; and the foresight of the company president who sent me to the CLNC® Certification Seminar. Vickie's CLNC® Certification Program was great, informative and certainly the beginning of my success.

My success has allowed my husband to retire and we have taken three fabulous vacations.

My $100,000 Tax Return Put Me Over the Moon with Joy

by Sharon Miller, RN, BSN, CLNC, Maryland

Hi Vickie, I just had to tell you the great news. I just finished my taxes and I am happy, no make that thrilled, no make that "over the moon with joy" to tell you that I earned more than $100,000. I went ahead and incorporated and named my CLNC® business when the work started coming in faster than I could keep up.

I just keep working hard trying to keep up with all of the work and make sure that I still put out top-quality work product. I was so happy when one of my attorney-clients forwarded my information to another law firm. I did a case for them and they were so happy with the "excellent CLNC® work product" that I provided that they immediately forwarded another case to me.

I have been keeping so busy and I absolutely love being able to work for myself. I still have the law firm that I first started working for. I have also gotten cases from the medical-malpractice attorneys, nursing home negligence and more. I am keeping so busy that I am going to have to start hiring CLNC® subcontractors. Luckily I met this incredible nurse and I convinced her to go through your CLNC® Certification Program, which she just recently completed. Now that she is a CLNC®

consultant, I am ready to ask her to subcontract with me on my huge case load.

I now have cases going to trial. I am working with three attorney-clients who are in the first round of trials and two attorney-clients in the second group of trials. These cases all need detailed chronological summaries – something that I have been providing to these law firms for deposition preps.

Anyway, I just thought I would let you know how happy I am that I became a Certified Legal Nurse Consultant[CM]. I love the way that I can combine my love and knowledge of nursing with my love of law. Thank you, Vickie, a hundred times over for helping me become a successful Certified Legal Nurse Consultant[CM]. You rock!

I hope my positive experiences will help other Certified Legal Nurse Consultants[CM] go for that BIG success. I feel honored to share my CLNC® successes.

I am keeping so busy that I am going to have to start hiring CLNC® subcontractors.

I combined my love and knowledge of nursing with my love of law.

My Legal Nurse Consulting Business Is the Ticket to Retiring in 5 Years

by Carol Riley, RN, MHA, CNAA, HFA, CLNC, Indiana

After five years as a Certified Legal Nurse Consultant[CM], my success was moderate, and I was staying busy part time. I had not been overly aggressive with marketing and had settled into the security of receiving cases from my regular attorney-clients on a "trickle in, trickle out" basis. I was enjoying the time to pursue my hobbies while still contributing to the family income and paying for my daughter's college tuition. Jordanne is in nursing school, and I felt good knowing my earnings would help place another nurse in the ranks by the time I was ready to retire.

You Never Know Where Your Next Referral Will Come From

Little did I know that my daughter would provide my best referral. Remember how Vickie tells us to market ourselves to anyone and everyone? As my story proves, you never know where your next referral will come from.

About a year ago Jordanne was at her part-time job in a local chain restaurant. One Friday night a nice looking young man wearing National Guard fatigues pulled up in a Jaguar. As his order arrived and she checked him out, she admired his Jaguar and commented that the National Guard must be doing well for him. At that he smiled and told her his real job was as a med-mal defense attorney. She nonchalantly replied, "My mother works with attorneys."

He asked what I did. When she told him I was a Certified Legal Nurse Consultant^CM, he almost dropped his food. He immediately started asking what kind of cases I specialized in and whether I had room in my caseload for more. He dug around but couldn't find a business card.

Fortunately, Jordanne had one of my cards in her wallet and gave it to him. He literally took a napkin, wrote down his personal email address, business and cell phone numbers, and asked her to have me call him ASAP. He had cases to send me.

She couldn't wait to get home and tell me about the encounter. It's been a long time since anyone wrote their number on a napkin for me!

Letters of Recommendation Are My Best Marketing Tool

The next evening I called him on his cell phone. It sounded like he was at a party, but he took the time to ask about my clinical experience, my legal nurse consulting experience and my availability. I learned he was with a big firm in a major city downstate.

He immediately offered an additional 33% if I could complete the case in two weeks.

On Monday I sent him my brochure, resume, letter of recommendation and work product samples.

By Thursday I hadn't heard from him. On Friday I nervously made that follow-up call Vickie stresses as essential to our success.

He answered his business phone himself. When I asked if he had any questions, he said he didn't. My heart sank. *Then* he added that he and his paralegal had just sorted through a "tabletop full of cases" to decide which ones they would send me.

I asked if he wanted to know what I charged, and he said, "Sure, but it doesn't matter. That letter of recommendation convinced me you have exactly the skills we need." He was referring to the letter from one of my attorney-clients, a well-known plaintiff attorney.

As Vickie says, a good letter of recommendation is one of your best marketing tools. This new defense attorney-client said he would make sure he didn't have to try any cases against "your plaintiff attorney" because he didn't want to go up against me as the opposing expert. I nearly fell out of my chair.

I'm Now on Track for Retirement – or a Jaguar

The cases started arriving the following week and the flood hasn't stopped. After receiving the first case, I emailed to advise him that I was available and to inform him of my hourly rate. He immediately offered an additional 33% if I could complete the case in two weeks. Needless to say, I met that deadline and enjoyed the premium. Since then I've been so busy I've had to use CLNC® subcontractors.

I can't believe my good fortune. My husband is astounded that my "little business" is making so much money. I just paid off my Jeep and bought a new quilting machine so I can enjoy my hobby in my spare time – even though I don't have as much spare time since my Certified Legal Nurse Consultant^{CM} practice took off. Oh well, the quilting machine will be there for my "real" retirement.

My goal is to retire in five years. With Vickie's advice and training, my CLNC® business is sure to make that retirement happen on schedule, leaving me professionally fulfilled and financially secure. You never know, I just might trade that Jeep for a Jag.

I've been so busy I've had to use CLNC® subcontractors.

How I Achieved Big City Success in a Small Town as a Certified Legal Nurse Consultant^{CM}

by Danita F. Deaton, RN, BA, CLNC, Texas

Most people think of my small town in Texas as just a blip on the map as they drive through to the Louisiana casinos. But I chose to settle here. Born in Sulphur, Louisiana, I grew up in Alaska, where I was a CPA for ten years, got my nursing degree in Denver and then moved to Southeast Texas.

I went directly into adult intensive care. I've worked numerous areas of nursing, including ER and management. I was director of nursing in a long term, extended care unit and I've done a lot of quality assurance, so I have a broad background in nursing and administration.

As nurses, we're here to do a job, and I think we should do it well, but the medical field has a lot of problems. I'm a patient advocate, and I knew there had to be a better way to help. I had seen information about the Institute's CLNC® Certification Seminar, and I had looked up Vickie Milazzo Institute on the Internet. I began thinking legal nurse consulting might be the road I was searching for. I contacted the Institute and received a packet, but I didn't follow through. I'm a world-class procrastinator.

Then I took a position as director of a neonatal intensive care unit. Because of my critical care background, my employer also talked me into being director of the telemetry department. Instead of wearing a pager 24/7, I was basically on call 48/14 in two different units. I finally left this extremely stressful job for PRN work in Houston.

In the meantime, I had remarried. I wanted to spend more time with my husband and my two-year-old grandson. I was dissatisfied with where nursing was going for me. I knew I had more to offer, and I didn't want to retire with a bad back. So I checked out Amway and Mary Kay and took a learn-at-home course in real estate.

I Decided Enough Was Enough

One day my daughter, who worked at a car wash, met an attorney bringing his Jaguar to be cleaned. She told him, "My mom's a nurse. She could help you with some cases."

The next thing I knew, this attorney phoned, asking me to review a couple of nursing home cases. I put in four hours at most on each of those cases. That felt great – I could do this. Yet despite follow-up, that attorney didn't call me back.

I decided enough was enough. I wasn't getting any younger, and I didn't want to work nights anymore. I found that packet from Vickie Milazzo Institute, read it through, decided I was going to do this and signed up for the VIP CLNC® Success System.

> *I decided I was going to do this and signed up for the VIP CLNC® Success System.*

> *At the CLNC® Certification Seminar, I felt like a few hundred light bulbs went off in my head.*

Vickie Inspired Me to Go for It

At the CLNC® Certification Seminar, I felt like a few hundred light bulbs went off in my head. I realized I hadn't done a fourth of what I could have done to help that attorney on those first two cases, and the money I received was nothing compared to what I could make. This was wonderful.

After the seminar I was so fired up, I decided to follow Vickie's advice and do something toward my new career every day. I spread out all of the materials from my VIP CLNC® Success System and marked my calendar. I worked out a budget. I hired a CPA and an attorney to incorporate my company. Both my CPA and my attorney gave me some referrals. I wrote the names in my *I Am a Successful CLNC® Success Journal*. Three weeks after receiving my CLNC® Certification, I was in business.

I kept looking at that *Success Journal*, at the quotes on each page. I knew I was going to do this, but besides being a procrastinator, I'm also a perfectionist. I didn't want to call those referrals until I had everything perfect. Finally, my attorney phoned and said, "Danita, you haven't called this guy yet. I told him to expect your call. He's waiting."

The CLNC® Mentors Guided Me to Success

The next day I phoned that attorney, met with him and took home a case. At first I just stared at the file. I didn't even have my intro letter written,

> *After the seminar I was so fired up, I decided to follow Vickie's advice and do something toward my new career every day.*

> *I phoned that attorney, met with him and took home a case.*

yet I had a case. Easy to say I could do it, easy to fake it while I was in the attorney's office, but now I had to deliver on my promise. I remembered those two early cases and never hearing back from the attorney. I couldn't let that happen again.

This time I had Vickie's VIP CLNC® Success System materials and unlimited CLNC® Mentoring. I called the Institute and described the case. The CLNC® Mentor said, "First, take a few deep breaths." After talking with her and with the attorney again, I wrote a 30-page report advising the attorney that the case was meritorious.

Meanwhile, I wrote my intro letter. Again, I called the Institute for help, and I put together a simple package with my resume, sample reports and a bulleted list of ten CLNC® services. A month after attending the CLNC® Certification Seminar, I mailed out my first six marketing packets.

The next week I was ready to send out six more packets, as Vickie encouraged us to do. Before I could leave to go to the post office, a paralegal from one of the big malpractice firms called. Two of their attorneys wanted to see me. I didn't want to say I was available anytime, and I was still working two nights a week, so I scheduled the interview on a day when I wouldn't be trying to sleep.

I walked into my interview wearing my nice black suit. Both attorneys had my packet on the table in front of them. When I asked why they called me, one attorney said, "We were impressed with your marketing package. It was

> *I mailed out six marketing packets. One of the big malpractice firms called. Two of their attorneys wanted to see me.*

very professional, with no grammatical errors, no misspellings." My package showed I had taken the time to do it right.

Vickie Helped Me Anticipate Every Question

In my briefcase I had the list of questions and answers Vickie had told us to expect in interviews. The attorneys' questions matched that list almost verbatim.

One of their biggest questions concerned my rates. When I said I charged $125 an hour, the first attorney said, "That's kind of high, don't you think?" I kept quiet, almost sitting on my hands, as Vickie advised.

After a few seconds, he said, "Tell me why I should pay you $125 an hour."

"Because I'm good at what I do," I said. When he asked what was the difference between me and a paralegal, I said, "Being a paralegal would be a step backward. I have an expertise, paralegals have an expertise and you have an expertise. I'm not an attorney, and you're not a nurse. That's why we can work together."

When we finished the interview, one attorney asked if I wanted to work for them full time. I said no, I could do more for them independently. He said he didn't have the case files but would get back to me in a few days.

I shook his hand, gave him another card and said, "I'll phone you in about ten days to see how

> *I had the list of questions and answers Vickie had told us to expect in interviews. The attorneys' questions matched that list almost verbatim.*

things are going. In the meantime, if you have any more questions at all, please call me."

As I started to leave, his partner said, "I do have a few more questions. Do you have time?" Not wanting to look desperate, I checked my watch, then agreed I had half an hour.

But I left without a case in hand. My heart fell to the floor. On the way home, I chalked it up to experience, but I kept telling myself, "It'll work, it'll work." Three days later, the firm's paralegal called to say they had four cases waiting for me to pick up.

I Was Instantly So Busy, I Didn't Know Where to Start

I arrived at their offices to find four boxes and a $3,000 retainer check. My heart rate was about 250. I actually had cases to work – and a check.

Before I could get out the door with the boxes, one attorney asked to see me about another case. In addition to my other CLNC® services, he needed an expert witness. I told him my fee for finding an expert, then remembered a friend who would be perfect. I gave him that name for free. He offered to pay, but I said, "No, this one's on me. You can pay for the next one."

Once again, I called the Institute. The CLNC® Mentor told me to pace myself, which I did. I finished the cases, and the attorneys were thrilled with my work.

The firm called to say they had four cases waiting for me. I arrived to find four boxes and a $3,000 retainer check.

Then I heard nothing for a couple of days, which felt like months. Then another attorney called with a "simple nursing home case" for me to review. I picked it up, spent a couple of hours reviewing it and called to tell him the case had merit. He asked me to put that in a memo.

This time I got out my CLNC® Certification course materials. Vickie has included everything I need. I used the memo form, typed up the memo and sent it off.

I Received 24 Cases from One Attorney All at Once

I was so busy with cases in November that my husband agreed I should do the legal nurse consulting full time and stop working at the hospital. Come December, all the cases were finished and no calls were coming in. In a major panic, I called the Institute. My CLNC® Mentor told me most attorneys don't do a lot during the holidays. That made sense. I decided not to worry. My husband and I went to California to see his family for Christmas. When we returned, I made my New Year's resolution to continue marketing, no matter what.

The first week of January, I received a call from the attorney who had hired me for those first two cases three years earlier. When I told him my new rates, he said, "That's kind of steep." Again, I sat on my hands. Finally, he said, "All right, I have a list of cases I want you to review."

I expected five or six cases at most. He gave me 24.

My Next Goal Is a Six-Figure Income

Vickie is so right when she says, "We are nurses and we can do anything!®" We can. We always sell ourselves short, but whatever we set our minds to, we can do. All I did was follow Vickie's advice, use her materials and ask to speak to a CLNC® Mentor whenever I panicked.

My husband and I are going to Hawaii next week. I don't have to check with anyone. As a nurse, I never could have achieved that feeling of independence and freedom.

In six months I've worked 36 legal nurse consulting cases. I'm on a roll now, and my next CLNC® goal is to make a six-figure income. With everything I've learned from Vickie, I know I can do it.

In six months, I've worked 36 legal nurse consulting cases. My CLNC® goal is to make a six-figure income. With everything I've learned from Vickie, I know I can do it.

> *I have
> so much
> money
> coming in,
> I don't
> know what
> to do
> with it.
> I thank
> Vickie from
> the bottom
> of my heart.*

With Vickie's Recipe I Made More Money in 2 Months as a Certified Legal Nurse Consultant^CM Than in 12 as a Hospital Nurse

by Pamela Erwin, RN, BSN, MS, CLNC, California

I love what I'm doing! In spite of, or actually because of, injuries and pain from a couple of car wrecks, I have achieved professional success and financial independence as a Certified Legal Nurse Consultant^CM. I've done just about everything in nursing – pediatrics, emergency trauma and cardiac intensive care.

While in the cardiac care unit, I also earned an MS in counseling and became interested in the healing benefits of alternative healthcare methods. I changed my lifestyle as well as my family's through diet, meditation, yoga and *tai chi*.

When injuries from a car accident sidelined me for six months, I took a more accommodating position as director of professional services for a girl's reformatory. Another wreck proved to be a real life-changing event. The injuries to my jaw, shoulder, neck and right arm forced me to move to a hot, dry climate.

Meanwhile, someone showed me literature from the Institute's CLNC® Certification Program. I was very impressed and thought, "Boy, they're on target. This is really interesting." Having served as an expert witness on a few occasions, I already knew how much attorneys didn't know about the medical details of cases.

Upon relocation, I had several attractive offers, but I couldn't work a normal 8- to 10-hour day. I realized that legal nurse consulting was my solution. I found the Institute's website and read up on the CLNC® Certification Program. Vickie's program really hit home with me. I became highly motivated to pursue a career as a Certified Legal Nurse Consultant^CM.

I got a couple of consulting jobs from friends of friends — I made $2,000 on one case and $5,000 on another.

If I Could Make Millions for Others, I Could Do It for Myself, Too

I knew I had the background to succeed as a CLNC® consultant, but I was scared. My biggest fear was financial. How could I become financially independent, especially in light of my physical limitations? I became determined to get past the pain from my injuries.

I was also fearful about being on my own and not being around my colleagues. Vickie's free CLNC® Mentoring Program was very helpful, and I knew its importance from my counseling background. Even today, I still call the Institute, especially when I have a challenging case.

Although I'd been consulting for two years, going from a fixed-salary to doing it all on my own was a big step for me. But I realized I'd consulted on six start-ups and made millions of dollars for others, so why couldn't I do it for myself? Of course, that's the theme of Vickie's message.

I ordered the CLNC® Certification Program and studied daily for three months, working at it like an eight-hour shift. I went through the course three times. When I took the exam, the Institute helped me get special accommodation to move around because I couldn't sit for that long. Actually, my arm was numb during the exam, and after I got home, I cried in pain – but I passed with flying colors.

I Marshaled One Case to Full-Time CLNC® Success

I was ready to go. I got a couple of consulting jobs from friends of friends – I made $2,000 on one case and $5,000 on another. My first big assignment came about because of my own door-to-door, out-of-the-phone-book efforts.

Two months after I submitted my marketing packet to one attorney, he called for an interview. After another two months he left a message on my answering machine. Two friends of his law firm's owner had been badly injured in a car wreck. They were in a hospital that had many malpractice lawsuits pending against it, and the owner was afraid his friends, both comatose, would not survive there. The attorney asked me to meet him and his boss at the hospital and review the situation, or as they put it, "marshal the case."

I went in daily and discovered that the care the accident victims were receiving was very poor. I could horrify you for an hour with what I saw and how I intervened. To make a long story short, both victims are okay, although one was in rehab for six weeks, and the case settled for a lot of money.

I never intended to be a full-time Certified Legal Nurse Consultant[CM], but I've been full time ever since this case. I started getting a case about every 10 days, and I've hired a CLNC® subcontractor to help. I'm so busy with my current attorney-clients, I don't have time for other law firms.

I made more money in two months as a CLNC® consultant than I made in 12 as a hospital nurse. I charge $150/hr. My attorney-clients often ask for my informal opinion about a medical situation in a case. These informal consultations are also billable at $150/hr.

I make sure my clients receive plenty of benefits from my CLNC® services. The attorneys know I'm a valuable asset to their efforts and have said so. I actually save them a lot of time and money by helping them establish a direction in a case or determine if a case is worth pursuing.

I give the attorneys a thorough grasp of the medical aspects vital to a case. I show them examples to help them relate to seemingly minor details that are actually life and death issues. Rather than just giving them a general understanding that

> *I made more money in two months as a CLNC® consultant than in 12 as a hospital nurse. I charge $150/hr.*

something is wrong, I try to give them a visceral response to the medical malpractice. That's when they really "get it" and can present a strong case.

Vickie's Recipe Gave Me Independence and Financial Success

My financial goals were to be able to support myself, live independently, not have to worry about my finances, be a philanthropist of sorts and put my kids through college. I also wanted my work to be honorable and ethical, and to uphold my values. In addition to the money, independence and opportunity to work from home, I love my professional relationships with my attorney-clients and the variety of CLNC® services I get to provide.

I attribute my success to my intentions, to focusing my positive energy. My nursing experience has helped a lot, and I have followed Vickie's advice like a recipe.

Although I've never met Vickie, I feel like she and I are two peas in a pod. Judging by her website, the things she's done and the way she talks, I can tell she's incredibly organized. Yet we also share an interest in *feng shui*, which tells me she's not all traditional. You need some untraditional thinking to succeed in this world.

I am very happy helping attorneys help patients who have been abused by the healthcare system. I know from firsthand experience there's a great need for this kind of work.

> *I started getting a case about every 10 days, and I've hired a CLNC® subcontractor to help. I'm so busy with my current attorney-clients, I don't have time for other law firms.*

I still have some of the pain and physical limitations that led me into this field, but I'm having fun now. I have so much money coming in, I don't know what to do with it. I thank Vickie from the bottom of my heart.

"In addition to the money, independence and opportunity to work from home, I love my professional relationships with my attorney-clients."

After Only 3 Months Following Vickie's System, I'm a Full-Time Certified Legal Nurse Consultant^{CM}

by Tanya Sanderson, RN, BSN, RCIS, CLNC, Tennessee

> *My CLNC® success happened faster than I imagined it could.*

> *Only one week after the CLNC® Certification Seminar I met with my first attorney-prospect and walked out of his office with two cases.*

My CLNC® success happened faster than I imagined it could. The CLNC® Certification Seminar and *NACLNC®* 2-Day Apprenticeship gave me everything I needed. I learned how to write the letters, mail them out, make the follow-up phone calls and get appointments with attorneys. I was totally prepared.

Vickie Taught Me Everything

I sent out eight letters the first time, then nine. I received so many cases, I had to hold off on further marketing until I got them under control. Not that they were really out of control. From the report writing section of the *NACLNC®* 2-Day Apprenticeship, I knew how to review cases for merit and write my reports. I've done several chronologies. Most of my cases are medical malpractice, but I've also done a workers' comp case.

When I first returned from the CLNC® Certification Seminar, I met with a business advisor. Everything he told me to do I had already learned from Vickie. My husband would talk to business people he knew, then ask me, "Did you do this?" I'd say, "Yes, honey. Vickie taught me everything."

I tell my attorney-clients that anytime I have a question I can't answer, I have unlimited access to 4,000 Certified Legal Nurse Consultants[CM] who have all the collective knowledge I could ever need. It's reassuring to know the CLNC® Mentors are there, too. When I encounter an issue, I'm always impressed with the depth and value of their answers and guidance.

Only one week after the CLNC® Certification Seminar I met with my first attorney-prospect and walked out of his office with two cases. I took that as a sign and turned in my resignation at the hospital.

I'm the Attorney's "Expert!"

When my first attorney-client found out I had resigned from my nursing job, he promised to do all he could to help my CLNC® practice grow. He's given me several cases and a referral. Another attorney has done the same.

I called one of these referrals and left a message, but didn't hear back. Then one day, on a whim, I stopped by her office. That turned out to be one of the most exciting events since I started my business.

"I'm so glad you came by," she said and mentioned the attorney who referred me. "When I asked him to help me on this case, he told me his expert would need to review it first."

Every day I love my new CLNC® business more. Weekends are spent with my family.

I was the expert. My attorney-client had called me an 'expert.'

A moment later it hit me – *I* was the expert. My attorney-client had called me an "expert."

My Husband Looks at Me Differently

Every day I love my new CLNC® business more. I work at home, take my daughter out to lunch and come and go as I please. Weekends are spent with my family. I attend Saturday-night ball games and never miss a Sunday at church. For the past two years at the hospital, I worked on Christmas Eve and Christmas Day, which are big events when you have small children. Now I'll never have to work another holiday.

My husband even looks at me differently. In many ways, I'm a country girl. I love gardening in my jogging pants with a bandana on my head and no makeup. Now I wear business suits, I get my hair done and wear makeup every day. I look and feel professional. Sometimes I catch my husband watching me as if I'm a new person in his life. He's my best friend, and he's always been respectful, but now he shows me a different kind of respect, an intellectual respect. I see that in my attorney-clients too, and it's nice.

Following Vickie's System, Any Certified Legal Nurse Consultant℠ Can Succeed

At the *NACLNC*® Conference, I realized how quickly my success had occurred. After being certified in October, I got started in December and by the end of February had built a flourishing CLNC® business.

All I did was take Vickie's advice – and follow it. Everything I learned in the CLNC® Certification Seminar and *NACLNC*® 2-Day Apprenticeship paid off. My money and my time were definitely well spent. Each day, I took one action step toward creating my business, even if it was only going to the office supply store and buying staples. Vickie said, "Just go for it," and I did.

I'll continue to go for it. As a nurse, I specialized in cardiology. Now I'm learning even more about other disease processes that I learned about in nursing school. Being a CLNC® consultant is an amazing new adventure.

Although I've already tucked away enough money to pay the bills for three months, I feel confident that the cases will never stop pouring in. I believe any Certified Legal Nurse Consultant^CM can be equally successful – you just have to follow Vickie's system and take one action step every day toward your CLNC® success just like Vickie teaches.

I got started in December and by the end of February had built a flourishing CLNC® business. All I did was take Vickie's advice – and follow it.

I Made $142,000 in My First Year as a Part-Time Certified Legal Nurse Consultant^{CM}

by Lynn Hydo, RN, MBA, CLNC, New York

I've worked in New York hospitals for 20 years, in surgical ICU and critical care. Before I became a Certified Legal Nurse Consultant^{CM}, I was already reviewing cases to help my boss. He took all the credit and enjoyed all the success. A colleague suggested I enroll in the CLNC® Certification Program and become an independent CLNC® consultant. I did, and since then, tremendous things have happened.

My CLNC® training taught me to focus. Instead of spending time on irrelevant research – looking for a needle in a haystack – I learned to get to the heart of a case quickly. I know how to single out the key elements. Attorneys appreciate this, and I've stayed busy completing a case a week. In my first year as a part-time CLNC® consultant, I did about 50 cases at an average of nearly $3,000 per case.

Caring for Attorneys the Way I Care for My Patients Keeps Them Coming Back

I've done a little marketing – business cards, Christmas cards, a few Christmas gifts to my biggest clients – but most of my business comes through referral. Word of mouth is the best. All it takes to generate referrals is giving your attorney-clients the same individualized care you'd give a patient.

If an attorney needs information on a particular product, disease or other subject, I can find it. For one of my cases I did extensive research on a rare germ found in a patient. But hands down, my most popular CLNC® service is the chronology – that's what I deliver most often.

If a case is time sensitive, I push it to the head of the queue. I can turn a case around in less than a week, working on it day and night, if that's what my attorney-client needs. Providing this kind of service wins me repeat business as well as good referrals.

I Used to Come Up Short Financially – Now I'm a Woman of Means

Succeeding as a CLNC® consultant takes perseverance, not only when business is good and you have more work than time, but also when your desk is empty and you wonder if you'll get another case.

Before I became a CLNC® consultant, I was doing all right financially, but occasionally I came up a little short when it was time to pay the mortgage. Now I'm a woman of means. The most exciting thing that's happened to me is watching that balance grow in my business bank account. I can hardly believe it's real – $142,000 – and I achieved this working just part time.

> *I finally have a bank account that makes me feel secure. What's more exciting than that?*

I know my business will get even better over time. When you do a good job, there's always another case around the corner. Someday I'll consider becoming a full-time CLNC® consultant, but for now part time is paying off big. I finally have a bank account that makes me feel secure. What's more exciting than that?

My most popular CLNC® service is the chronology. Providing this kind of service wins me repeat business as well as good referrals.

I Make the Rules and I've Tripled My Income as a Legal Nurse Consultant in Florida

by Colleen Galligan, RN, BSN, CDDN, CLNC, Florida

What's amazing about the CLNC® Certification Program is that Vickie teaches you absolutely everything you need to know and gives you all the tools to succeed. The most important thing she told me was to use the CLNC® Mentors.

I can walk into an attorney's office knowing nothing about the case and come out with the assignment. Then I contact Vickie Milazzo Institute, and a CLNC® Mentor is always able to help me sort it out. I ask all my questions, even if I think they're stupid, get the answers and the attorney thinks I'm brilliant.

The other thing Vickie told us was to stick together. If everybody succeeds, then we all do better. This is the only job I've ever had where people in the business really want to help each other. You won't find that anyplace else.

I relocated from New York to Florida. Unemployment can be a great motivator, so I decided to go for it all the way as a Certified Legal Nurse Consultant℠ in Florida. I figured out what I had to earn to replace my nursing salary, $58,000 a year, with my 20 years of experience in developmental disabilities. To equal that as a

> *I work only 25 to 30 hours a week, and I earn three times what I'd be making as a full-time, 60-hour-a-week nurse.*

> *I make the rules. I can do high-quality work in my pajamas. It's my choice, and that's unbelievable freedom.*

CLNC® consultant, I only needed to work six to eight hours a week. I did the math three times to believe it, and I knew it was attainable.

I Creatively Turned "No" into "Yes"

I sent out introductory letters and got creative in responding to "no": "It's been nice meeting you. Maybe I'll see you across the table. Do you know anyone else I should talk to?"

Eventually, "no" started turning into "yes." The first time that happened was one of the most fun days I can remember. As I walked into the courtroom to sit in on a plaintiff case, I recognized the attorney across the table. Not long before, he had told me I overcharged and he would never be interested. When he spotted me, the expression on his face was priceless. The next day he called. It's fun to hear "no" turn to "yes, please"!

I'm proud to say that my first three clients are still my best clients. I landed them by sending out letters, knocking on doors, showing up and being nice to paralegals. I know my clients need and appreciate my CLNC® services.

Once my CLNC® business took off, I got into networking, and my business multiplied even faster. I'm the only CLNC® consultant in my networking group, and each week I meet at least 50 people. Now instead of knocking on an attorney's front door, I go in through the back door – by referral from a golf partner, bridge partner or next-door neighbor. Once I get in with one attorney, they send me to others.

I got into networking, and my business multiplied even faster. Once I get in with one attorney, they send me to others.

After Only a Year I'm Free to Take Off Whenever I Want

A year after moving to Florida, I work only 25 to 30 hours a week, and I earn three times what I'd be making as a full-time, 60-hour-a-week nurse. I provide my own benefits, but the perks are huge. I make the rules. I can do high-quality work in my pajamas here in Florida. It's my choice, and that's unbelievable freedom.

After spending a lot of years attached to a beeper and cell phone, I love the fact that I don't carry a beeper. Anyone who wants me can leave a message and I'll get back to them.

If I want to work 16 hours a day, I can. If I want to take off in the middle of the day and go see a movie, I can do that, too. When I lived in Manhattan, I never had time to see a Broadway show. Now, if my husband comes home and says, "It's a beautiful day. Let's go to the beach," I can go. I have three cruises and two additional vacations planned for the coming year.

If I want to take off in the middle of the day and go see a movie, I can.

I have three cruises and two additional vacations planned.

Through Referrals I'm Making Money Faster Than I Ever Expected

I thought I'd be doing medical malpractice cases, but two personal injury attorneys opened their doors to me and gave me my first cases. I figured out what they needed and gave it to them. The basis of my business is a report I developed for one of my first personal injury clients. As we discussed his case, I could tell he didn't quite understand

I'm making more money faster than I ever expected, and I love it.

what I was saying about my CLNC® services. I told him, "It sounds like you want the good, the bad and the ugly," just as Vickie teaches. He replied, "That's exactly what I want." He called the next week to say, "I love that report. It's great."

I later learned that he shared my report with other attorneys. One morning while I was still in my pajamas, I got a call from an attorney I'd never met. He said, "I need one of those GBUs." I didn't know what he was talking about, so I asked how he got my name. That's when I figured it out – he wanted the good, the bad and the ugly.

Now I have lots of attorneys asking for my "GBU" reports. They're three to five pages long and take five to ten hours to complete. I do five or ten GBUs a week, and they're really fun.

My CLNC® business didn't develop exactly as I had planned. I do personal injury, not medical malpractice. I'm making more money faster than I ever expected, and I love it. I love the work, I love the freedom I have here in Florida, I love my clients and I love Vickie Milazzo Institute for showing me how to make it happen.

My First CLNC® Retainer Check Was More Than an Entire Month's RN Salary

by Jamescia Hambrick, RN, BSN, CCRN, CLNC, Nevada

> *My first retainer was more than I made as a nurse for an entire month.*

My mother and grandmother were both nurses, so I was third-generation. In my 23rd year as a nurse, I started wondering what was next. Single, with grown-up children, I was free to take the next step. And I knew I wanted to go back to school – maybe get my masters or become a nurse anesthetist, but nothing inspired me.

Early in my career, my mom gave me some really good advice. "When you work in a hospital," she said, "don't limit yourself to one particular area. Learn as many specialties and get involved in as much as possible, so the hospital administrators feel they can't get along without you." That's what I did.

One of my instructors in nursing school, a person I'm still really close to, tells me I was always an overachiever. From day one, options and variety were important to me. When the opportunity arose to float to a different unit or to participate on committees, I was the first to raise my hand. Because of that, I've worked in many areas of nursing, from pediatrics to burns to critical care.

Grabbing Hold of an Unexpected Opportunity Changed My Life

In college, I had a lot of girlfriends who went to law school. Two years ago, one of my close friends was running for vice president of the National Bar Association, and I helped with her campaign, including attending the convention. I couldn't sit in on many of the classes or symposiums because I was busy helping my friend, but I acquired an interest in the legal side of business as I sat in the background, listening.

My friend invited me to her inauguration in Washington, D.C., where I attended a couple of the balls. I also attended other events, including the National Bar Association convention, and this time I was free to enjoy the seminars and symposiums related to medical fields. During the luncheon, most of the attorneys assumed I was also an attorney. When I clarified that I was a nurse, they seemed suddenly interested.

"Are you a legal nurse consultant?" they asked. Immediately after lunch, I went to my hotel room, googled legal nurse consulting, quickly researched the topic, and found that Vickie Milazzo Institute was offering the CLNC® Certification Program in Las Vegas where I live. With my varied nursing experience, I felt this was a job I could do because I could service many different attorneys and review all kinds of cases. Vickie's CLNC® Certification Program was affordable, and since I had so many contacts in the legal world, how could I pass up the opportunity?

A Life-Changing Event Almost Changed My Mind

Vickie Milazzo Institute's CLNC® Certification Seminar was scheduled to start on October 21st. Then, on October 3rd, my mom passed away. My mom and I were close, so I had a hard time, but remembering she was the one who encouraged me to keep learning, I knew I had to attend the CLNC® Certification Program.

During one of the sessions, Vickie talked about starting her legal nurse business in honor of her mom, after her mother passed from cancer. I immediately started bawling. People around me asked, "Are you okay?" "Yes, absolutely," I said, because despite my tears, I felt like my mom was saying, "Jamescia, you're doing the right thing. You're going to be good at this." Later, when I explained to Vickie and told her how much I appreciated her talking about her mom, she hugged me. What more did I need in the way of confirmation?

The Realities of Launching My CLNC® Business Stimulated Me to Think Bigger

Right after signing up for the CLNC® Certification Program, I informed my attorney contacts that I would be starting my business as a Certified Legal Nurse Consultant℠. Then immediately after passing the test, I launched my CLNC® business, set up a home office, and created my CV, which I sent to the Vickie Milazzo

Currently, I have about 15 attorney-clients.

Vickie's CLNC® Certification Program was affordable, and since I had so many contacts in the legal world, how could I pass up the opportunity?

The travel and the excitement of meeting new people are part of what I love about being a CLNC® consultant.

Institute for CLNC® Mentoring. The Institute responded right away, offering excellent advice.

All of this helped me to think bigger than a typical RN salary. Much bigger.

One of my struggles, however, was learning to delegate. I would work at the hospital during the day, then come home and be up until 1:00am tending to the many little details required for starting and marketing my CLNC® business. It began to exhaust me.

Finally, I hired a personal assistant to help with things like going to the post office, putting together promotional packets and delivering tins of popcorn to my attorney-clients at Christmas. Taking that step has kept me from being overwhelmed.

Seizing the Day Turned an Opportunity Into Real Money

Recently, a Las Vegas hospital was all over the news when a patient they had been treating, after giving birth to premature twins, was discovered to have tuberculosis. Unable to diagnose her illness, they sent her to UCLA, where she died. The autopsy revealed TB and the twins were also positive for TB, so there was a huge exposure in the Las Vegas hospital. Luckily, I wasn't employed there.

A respiratory therapist I once worked with, who's also a Facebook friend, knew the attorney who was filing a class action lawsuit against the hospital. My friend, seeing that I'd started my

CLNC® business, contacted me, gave me the attorney's name and said I should talk to him.

Not one to pass up an opportunity, I immediately phoned the next morning and set up an appointment with the attorney for the following week. One of the partners of the law firm met with me and asked a lot of questions about TB. Afterward, he told his partners, "I want to sign this woman to work on the case." They hired me that day. When the attorney handed me my first retainer check, I wanted to jump up and scream. I managed to keep my composure but was so excited that as soon as I was alone in my car, I yelled, "This is it!" (The check was more than an entire month's RN salary!)

I'm making over $10,000 a week.

A short time later, the attorney was doing community outreach near the hospital to educate people about tuberculosis. I wrote a research paper for him and he invited me to attend the afternoon event. His talk was scheduled for about three hours. People could receive the information, and find out if they were at risk. Listening to him speak, I had to interject some clarifications, because the attorney wasn't saying things quite correctly. He asked me to come up and speak in front of this large group of people. I was shaking inside, but I did it.

So far, 172 people are plaintiffs in the lawsuit against the hospital. The case is huge, and I'm the primary Certified Legal Nurse Consultant^{CM}. When the attorney calls or texts me, "I need information ..." on this or that, he knows I'll get it for him.

I project making $100,000 my first year.

Becoming a Certified Legal Nurse Consultant^{CM} Took Me Out of the Hospital and Into the World

Maybe the signal went out in the universe, because right after signing that first contract, I got calls from other attorneys. "Can you do this?" "Yes." I responded immediately. I make a point of getting back to people right away, and I give my attorney-clients a quick turnaround time. All of this came about in less than three months. Currently, I have about 15 attorney-clients.

I have a friend in Detroit who is a district court judge. After hearing that I started my CLNC® business, she invited me to come out for five days to meet with attorneys and to also attend six holiday parties with her. Having run for the Supreme Court a couple of years earlier, this judge is well known in her city.

I love dressing for formal events. Choosing colors that attracted attention, and intentionally carrying a clutch that held my brochures and business cards, I set out to let people know who I was, a Certified Legal Nurse Consultant^{CM}. At one point, I confess to being a little bit "star struck," when I spied a beautiful personal injury attorney that I'd seen in TV commercials and on billboards all over Detroit. She had an entourage with her. While setting appointments, I researched her and made an appointment at her firm for the following day.

While the judge and I were at coat check, this attorney came up to say hello, and after she and the judge exchanged greetings, she wanted to know who I was. She hugged me and said, "I can't wait to meet with you tomorrow." People who saw me hugging her must have wondered, "Who is that woman?" For me, it was another "This is it!" moment.

One of the many good things that happened on that trip is that I was invited to return to Detroit for a Barrister's Ball. The travel and the excitement of meeting new people are part of what I love about being a CLNC® consultant.

I Want It All and I'm Making It Happen as a CLNC® Consultant

One of the things I decided during the CLNC® Certification Program is that I want CLNC® subcontractors. I want to be out there marketing, traveling, attending various events and growing my CLNC® business. I've already contacted some of the nurses who were in class with me. Their CVs and resumes are in my files, ready to go. They're excited about working together, and so am I.

Creating relationships is my strong suit. I constantly send emails and updates to my attorney-clients. I'm also working on a newsletter, and my attorney-clients are good about communicating with me, as well.

I'm so glad I took Mom's advice early on to seize every opportunity available to me in nursing. Receiving my first retainer check opened my eyes to the incredible possibilities available to me as a

Vickie Milazzo, you and your course have truly been a blessing.

I exhibited at a legal conference as a CLNC® consultant and landed my largest case.

Certified Legal Nurse Consultant℠. The number on that check was more than I made as a nurse for an entire month, even after 23 years, so I knew starting my CLNC® business was the right decision.

I just exhibited at a legal conference as a CLNC® consultant in Atlanta and landed a case with 16,000 pages of records. It's my largest case and I'm making over $10,000 a week. If everything keeps going as it has for the last three months, I project making $100,000 my first year, and quite possibly, a lot more. (Quite a bit more than an RN job salary, that's for sure!)

Thanks to my mom for encouraging me and to Vickie Milazzo for helping me make it happen. You and your course have truly been a blessing.

How a Certified Legal Nurse Consultant^CM Can Become the Attorney's 'Go-To' Person

by Debbie L. Mitro, RN, BSN, CWON, CLNC, New York

> *I've had 12 cases and the attorney keeps calling with different requests.*

Ask me about pressure ulcers – I can tell you anything you want to know. It's what I've done for 15 years, so I know it inside and out, and it's where I've gotten the bulk of my cases. I'm also good with falls, acute care and some long term care, but pressure ulcers – that's my field. I will go up against anybody, anywhere, anytime.

I started consulting with attorneys immediately after graduating from Vickie Milazzo Institute's Certified Legal Nurse Consultant^CM Certification Program. My daughter-in-law is a real estate attorney. They have to keep up their continuing legal education (CLE) credits, so she said, "Come to this conference. You can sponsor the coffee and Danish. Your name will be there on a plaque, and you can chat with the attorneys during breaks."

About three-quarters through the meeting, I was asked to speak for five minutes. My daughter-in-law said, "Remember, attorneys don't want to be there. These are not billable hours. So whatever you do, get in, get to the point, get out and make an impression," – the same thing Vickie tells us in the CLNC® Certification Program. This event gave me the courage to call the event coordinator and say, "I'd like to speak to the attorneys at one of your meetings. I have a number of topics, but I'm especially knowledgeable on pressure ulcers."

She said, "Hmmm, I don't know. Let me pass this along." She got back to me with, "That's a great idea," and invited me to speak to 20 attorneys in Syracuse and 40 attorneys in Buffalo. I recently spoke again in Buffalo, also on pressure ulcers. I walked away with four great leads.

Consulting on Medical-Related Cases Has Stretched Me

In nursing things are quick – you have a low potassium reading, you supplement it and move on to the next problem. In the CLNC® world, everything moves slower, which was an eye-opener for me.

I've had 12 cases so far, and only two have closed. The attorney keeps calling with different requests on one case (involving a schizophrenic) that is approaching trial. And I confess, this case has stretched me a bit.

The plaintiff attended an adult daycare center from 9:00am to 1:00pm, Monday through Friday. He had behavioral, hygiene and combative-abusive issues. During the course of his illness he became a diabetic and also developed MS. Periodically, if he had to walk for an extended time, he used a wheelchair. Progression was to the point that he was having trouble swallowing.

> "I came up with 360 deposition questions. The attorney was extremely pleased."

One day at daycare, he choked on a chicken sandwich he wasn't supposed to have. The daycare staff knew this wasn't a type of food he should eat, but he sent a buddy to buy it. He choked and is currently in a vegetative state. At present, he's in a long term care facility, but his mom would like to bring him home.

As the case has progressed, I've had to research standards of care for adult daycare centers. The daycare facility provided diabetic instruction from a nurse who was on staff Monday through Friday. I looked through her employment record. This woman didn't take many days off. Unfortunately, she did take this day off.

Without her, nobody assisted the choking patient until the paramedics arrived. No one was trained to do what might possibly have helped this man, such as: *Get the stuff out of his throat! Do the Heimlich on him!*

I listened to some of the verbiage from the 911 call. "We don't know how to do that. How do you do that?" The operator said, "Just put him on his side," and they responded, "We can't do that. He's in a wheelchair. " And, "We don't want to touch him. Foam is coming from his mouth."

My job was to research all that happened that day, how and why, which I did.

> *I've never had an issue with charging $125 an hour.*

Back to the *Core Curriculum for Legal Nurse Consulting®* Textbook

About six months later the attorney called. "There are six defendants," he said. "I'd like you to write deposition questions for all six." He was planning to interview the fire department, the paramedics, the social worker on staff, director of the facility, and others. Okay…except…I'd never written deposition questions before.

After referring back to Vickie Milazzo Instititute's *Core Curriculum for Legal Nurse Consulting®* textbook, I realized, Yes, I can do this. Once I was on a roll with each question, I would think, What about this? And this? Then I had to do research. For example, EMTs use specific equipment to verify oxygenation, the carbon dioxide in his blood, things like that, so I had to educate myself. In the end, I came up with 360 questions. The attorney was extremely pleased.

What's interesting is that I'd never met this attorney. During all the months we worked together, everything was by phone, email or text message. He asked me to come in as he was preparing to take depositions and wanted to go over everything together.

This was my opportunity to meet him in person and get to know his staff, so I wore my power suit. Vickie would be proud. We made such a good connection that when I was leaving, he said, "You know, Debbie, you're my go-to person."

I smiled and calmly thanked him, but inside I was screaming…Yes!!!

The Reward of Being Appreciated by Attorneys Is Exciting

Six months went by, with two major attorneys working on this case. As they're on the way to court for jury selection, I get a call.

"I need you to research the life expectancy of a person in a vegetative state, plus with diabetes, plus with hypertension, plus with this, this and this." I received the call on Thursday. He finished by saying, "I need it all by Monday."

So I buried myself in the case and got it done. By Sunday night, I had the information he needed. I then emailed it to him so he'd have a chance to look at it Sunday night. Monday morning, I called and went over everything. He was due in court at 11:00am. He was happy. As I said, this case challenged me, but the outcome is going to be good.

A different attorney from the Syracuse conference hired me for a nursing home case. Naturally, I was thrilled that I attended. This was a case that settled, and at 8:00pm one night I received a call from the attorney. Driving to Vermont, he apparently had tried to reach me several times, but we kept missing each other. When we finally connected, he said, "I was not going to leave a message or email you or text. I wanted to tell you in person. Because of your

> *You can be a Certified Legal Nurse Consultant*CM *from your dining table or from a wheelchair.*

My gosh, do you make money!

knowledge, your work product and how you helped me on this case, we had a very favorable outcome. I really appreciate your involvement."

That was the jolt, the big pat on the back, that made me believe, *Oh, my goodness, I can do this.* I've never had an issue with charging $125 an hour. The attorneys always come back with, "Your fees sound fine, here's what we need." I send my invoice and receive a check in the mail a few weeks later. Payment has never been a problem.

I tell my RN friends, *You can do this.* Part time, full time – you can be a Certified Legal Nurse Consultant^{CM} from your dining table or from a wheelchair – and my gosh, do you make money!

How My New Favorite Word Reeled in 4 New Cases as a Certified Legal Nurse Consultant^{CM}

by Kim Anable, RN, MSN, Ed, CLNC, Texas

> *One or two attorneys can keep you busy.*

After completing my master's degree, I knew I didn't want to teach nursing. I'd previously seen an advertisement for Vickie Milazzo Institute's CLNC® Certification Program and I couldn't stop thinking about it. The idea of using what I already knew in a more interesting way appealed to me.

Finally, a year later, the timing seemed right. My husband was on active duty and we were moving. Why not make the change complete? So we finished moving on Friday and I started the CLNC® Certification Program on Monday.

Three months later, I exhibited with a couple of Certified Legal Nurse Consultants^{CM} at a national legal conference. There were 750 attorneys present and I intended to talk to as many as possible. At one point while standing at our display, I introduced myself to an attorney sitting nearby. When he asked, "So what do you do?" I jumped right in with my 30-second elevator speech as if my client list was huge. "I take all those medical records and whittle them down to concise information for my attorney-clients." He then asked, "Can you do chronological timelines?" I responded with my new favorite word, "Absolutely!" His response, "Perfect. Do you have an example?" Of course, I did. Hadn't Vickie taught me to be prepared? I emailed the chronological timeline samples to the attorney's office, then telephoned him to follow up. After a brief discussion, he said, "Kim, I'll make your eyes swim."

I Learned to Roll with It

The first time an attorney-client critiques your work, it feels personal. The attorney sits there picking it apart, saying, "I don't like this," or "That's not right." And you're thinking, *Oh, but I put my heart and soul into this.* That's when I'd remember Vickie's advice, "It's not personal; it's business."

My first medical malpractice case was scary. The attorney wanted me to find a testifying expert, but after reviewing the files, I knew he didn't have a case. What if telling him his case was nonmeritorious caused me to lose his business? One or two attorneys can keep you busy, but the more you have, the safer you feel.

He had already signed my contract, so I could find him a testifying expert and let the expert break the bad news. But I needed to be honest. So I said, "If I find you an expert, there are questions I want him to answer for you, as these are the issues in your case that concern me." The attorney

> *I had four new cases on my desk.*

> *When they walk in from school, my office light goes off. I'm available to them.*

was grateful for my candid advice and was glad he hadn't filed yet.

Later, I exhibited with a CLNC® Marketing Mentor from Vickie Milazzo Institute at another legal conference. Several attorneys were talking about "TBI." They were looking for help with a case. They asked me, "Can you help out?" I could hear Vickie's voice: *You have to always be marketing.* So I smiled and uttered my favorite word, "Absolutely."

After the attorneys went to their next session, I turned to the CLNC® Marketing Mentor and said, "What the heck is a TBI?" TBI means traumatic brain injury. In the context of a hospital, I know what traumatic brain injury is, but in the legal context I didn't recognize the abbreviation.

Nevertheless, I was learning the ropes. The point is to put yourself out there. Take the case, *then* figure out what to do with it. I left that legal conference with 25 attorney contacts. That was on a Thursday. On Saturday, I emailed every one of them. On Monday, I had four new cases on my desk.

The Full Spectrum of Medical-Related Cases Is Fascinating

Right now I'm working on the most fascinating case I've had so far as a Certified Legal Nurse Consultant℠. The patient, a 35-year-old male, was in a motor vehicle accident which turned out to be a red herring. His attorneys were pursuing

> *Getting to see the whole spectrum is fascinating to me.*

the case as medical malpractice because after the accident the patient was diagnosed as having a copper deficiency. When the attending physicians administered copper it aggravated his symptoms. He didn't have a copper deficiency; he had Wilson's disease, a condition of having too much copper in the system.

Wilson's disease is an obscure double-genetic malady. Both parents have to be carriers, and only one in 30,000 births result in Wilson's disease, so not a lot of people have it. Prior to the accident the patient had not been diagnosed with Wilson's disease.

This case was fascinating to me because I had worked in the emergency department with someone who had Wilson's disease. In an effort to better understand copper deficiency, I had to do a lot of interesting research.

This case was different because I got to see it from the time the patient entered the medical system until the time damages occurred. Hindsight, as they say, is always 20/20. If you look at each piece of this case individually it's challenging to see the problem, whereas looking back through the records it becomes apparent. Getting to see the whole spectrum is fascinating to me.

I Have Amazing Freedom as a Certified Legal Nurse Consultant^{CM}

While teaching I worked five days a week, 7:30am-4:30pm, plus the hours I spent preparing for the next lecture and grading papers in the evenings. That didn't leave much time to spend with my boys. Now, when they walk in from school, my office light goes off. I'm available to them. One son is a gymnast and another is in the marching band. I go to all their events.

Yet they know that when I'm in my office with the door shut and my light on, they're not supposed to bother me. As a Certified Legal Nurse Consultant^CM, I work pretty much from 9:00am to 3:00pm, six days a week, and occasionally I'm called to lecture which keeps me active in nursing.

That attorney I met in Las Vegas who needed chronological timelines was good to his word. We talked in October and by the end of that month I had my first case. In November I billed more than $13,000. In December I billed well over 200 hours.

With money coming in I can do whatever I want to do. If I choose to accept a new case or a new series of litigation, fine. Or I can choose not to. That's where my strategic alliance comes in. The Certified Legal Nurse Consultants^CM I've become close to since the CLNC® Certification Seminar exchange referrals with me, and I also hire them as CLNC® subcontractors. Currently I'm handing off about 40 hours of overflow each month. This kind of freedom is amazing.

And yes, that attorney gave me so much work, he did make my eyes swim. Absolutely!

> *I also hire CLNC® subcontractors. Currently I'm handing off about 40 hours of overflow each month.*

> *The kind of freedom is amazing.*

Use Vickie's Proven Strategies for Your Own CLNC® Success

I Love Defining My Legal Nurse Consulting Success on My Own Terms

by Leana Peterson-Leaf, RN, CLNC, Illinois

> *I am making money, I feel successful and I love it. I feel stimulated and enthusiastic about my future.*

In high school I dreamed of traveling the world and unraveling mysteries untold. I wanted to be an investigative reporter. My only problem was that I was too shy to talk to strangers. So I went into nursing school to make a difference. Ironically, I found the courage not only to talk to strangers, but to ask them the most embarrassing questions about their bodily functions.

Over the course of my nursing career, I went from proud new nurse paying my dues on the night shift, to the top of the pay scale in hemodialysis. After spending more than 15 years in this specialty, and weathering the storms of managed care and downsizing, I found myself underpaid, overworked and undervalued. I was traveling the path I had most resisted, becoming a burned out nurse.

My CLNC® Certification Launched My Invigorating Trip to Success

For a number of years, I'd been planning to become a legal nurse consultant, but my plans were cast in Jello. Then I learned about Vickie Milazzo Institute's CLNC® Certification Program, and I had, as Oprah would say, my "Aha!" moment. I knew that Vickie Milazzo Institute's program was based on sound, ethical business practices and it is delivered with integrity. I had fortitude, persistence and faith in myself and in Vickie's principles. How could I fail if I applied those principles?

Becoming a Certified Legal Nurse Consultant^{CM} was my first step toward success. The trip has been invigorating.

When I started my consulting business, I defined success in measurable amounts of money. I quickly learned the *most* gratifying rewards are not tangible. Success comes when you least expect it, and it is not always what you expect.

Success #1: I Have the Best of Both Worlds

My first case was a large medical malpractice suit in a specialty I considered my greatest weakness, cardiac. I took the case anyway. Three hospitals were involved, and all the records were mixed together. It took me six hours just to put them in order. You can imagine how pleased my attorney-client was when I gave him a full report in just 32 pages, including a great deal of research.

This was my first success: Realizing I had fulfilled my dream of being a nurse *and* an investigative reporter. I have the best of both worlds.

Success #2: Self-Respect Is the Best Success of All

The attorney loved my report. His only question was, "What does CCU stand for?" I couldn't believe it. Here was an attorney getting ready to litigate a million-dollar suit, and he didn't even know what CCU means. I told myself, if he has the guts, I have the guts. That was my second success: Respecting and valuing my own abilities.

Success #3: Going for It Makes Everything Else Possible

At first, I practiced part-time as a CLNC® consultant, working approximately 20 hours a week while maintaining my full-time home health position and raising four teenagers. I quickly learned I could not devote the attention my CLNC® practice required. Following up with contacts and implementing the many ideas rolling around in my head became difficult.

> *I had fulfilled my dream of being a nurse and an investigative reporter. I have the best of both worlds.*

My husband, a businessman and most supportive partner, said, "Quit your job when you feel the time is right. I'm behind this all the way." That was all I needed to hear. Despite fearing loss of income, change of lifestyle and mostly failure, I stuck my neck out. My third success was finding the courage to go for it.

Success #4: My Value Lies in How I Think and What I Know

I have now been in business for only three years, but the personal and professional achievement I have experienced far exceeds anything I could have imagined. I am intellectually challenged by each new case, stepping out of my box to research and explore unknown territory.

When one regular client gives me a case, he often says, "It's yours. You tell me what to do." This kind of respect is a far cry from being valued for how much I can physically do in an eight-hour shift and how much of my personal time I am willing to give beyond the call of duty. This is my fourth success: I am valued and respected for how I think and what I know.

The Ultimate Success: I'm *Feeling* Successful Doing What I Love

Today, I am making money, I feel successful and I love it. I'm reaching out to attain goals and learning every day. Once again, I feel stimulated and enthusiastic about my future.

The personal and professional achievement I have experienced far exceeds anything I could have imagined.

I am valued and respected for how I think and what I know.

As I write this CLNC® Success Story, I'm sitting here in my bathrobe and slippers with my hair a mess. My kids are off to school and my dog is lying on the floor next to me. Around 9:00am the phone will start ringing, and I will be talking to clients who call me because they value my knowledge and expertise.

I am enjoying every step of this journey, both the challenges and the successes, because I am in control of my future. There are no failures in this business. If I don't get the new client, so what? I move on. There are lots of attorneys out there. Failures are merely learning experiences that lead to the next success, and the next.

The moral of my story is this: Doing what you love *is* success. Success is not defined by fortune alone. It doesn't come while you're looking for it. It comes unexpectedly while you're filling the needs of your clients. It arrives in the moment you discover the key to your case and put the last piece of the puzzle in place.

My advice to aspiring Certified Legal Nurse Consultants^{CM}: Stick your neck out and get busy failing – I mean, learning – so you too can succeed – on your own terms. Enjoy your journey to CLNC® success, because this journey truly has no end.

I am enjoying every step of this journey, both the challenges and the successes, because I am in control of my future.

In Just 8 Months I've Increased My Income 70% as a Certified Legal Nurse Consultant^{CM}

by Lori Lynn, RN, CLNC, Michigan

I first saw an ad for the CLNC® Certification Program in a nursing magazine about five years ago. What sparked my interest was the $125-plus per hour consulting fee I could earn. I have enjoyed nursing for 20 years, but I knew I didn't want to grow old being a hospital nurse. I was feeling a little dissatisfied with the politics, the bureaucracy, the increased patient loads and the administrative problems. Yet if I went to work in a doctor's office or outside the hospital, I felt I would never achieve some of my goals such as traveling. I wanted to increase my income and further my career but stay in a field related to nursing.

I called Vickie Milazzo Institute and requested my free information packet. When the information packet arrived, I read the free *CLNC® Success Stories* book and found it fascinating and exciting. These were nurses like me who became Certified Legal Nurse Consultants^{CM}. Even in the midst of trials and tribulations in their personal lives, they had triumphed and were now successful CLNC® consultants.

For a couple of years I entertained the idea of becoming a CLNC® consultant, but I was going through a divorce, I had an ill parent and this was a trying time in my life. I knew I needed emotional energy to focus on the CLNC® business.

Finally, three years later, my boyfriend, who's a very successful businessman, encouraged me to get certified. Last May I attended the CLNC® Certification Seminar and the *NACLNC*® 2-Day Apprenticeship that immediately followed.

I firmly believe that if I had not done the Apprenticeship, I wouldn't be where I am today. It prepared me to go out and market myself. As a nurse, I was so accustomed to serving and helping people that I wasn't used to selling myself. The Apprenticeship program gave me the extra boost of confidence and all the tools I needed to leap into the marketing aspect of my CLNC® business.

In Just 8 Months I Met All My Goals and Increased My Income 70%

When I got home, I started formulating a business plan with one-month, two-month and three-month goals. Like Vickie taught me, I began taking baby action steps every day. One of those baby steps was telling at least three people what I did. When my profession came up in the course of conversation, a lot of people didn't know what Certified Legal Nurse Consultants℠ do. I would explain, and they'd say, "I know an attorney" or "I have a neighbor who's an attorney." This easy networking is directly related to my success today.

Within only eight months, I have increased my income by 70%.

Other nurses have been curious, and I tell them that Vickie Milazzo Institute offers the only program that helps you flourish as a legal nurse consultant.

I also set a goal to be successful in my CLNC® business by my birthday, and on my birthday I got my first case. Now, I'm retired from the hospital because I couldn't juggle my hospital work with all my CLNC® assignments. That was another goal I met.

I feel like an investigative reporter. I get to look at medical records, piece together what happened and figure out the puzzle. That's fascinating. And within only eight months, I have increased my income by 70%. It's been an exciting journey.

Vickie Is an Incredible Role Model for Me and My CLNC® Business

Vickie is an awesome woman and she's really worked hard to get where she is. Yet she's actually one of us. Her teaching style is fresh, down to earth and easy to follow. She's highly motivating and encouraging. During the CLNC® Certification Seminar I found myself just waiting for every word that came out of her mouth. From the time I got certified last May until the *NACLNC®* Conference in March, I was counting the days. I know I wouldn't be here today without her VIP CLNC® Success System.

Legal nurse consulting is a specialized field. After the CLNC® Certification Seminar and the *NACLNC®* 2-Day Apprenticeship, I felt fully prepared to put on that power suit and shake hands with that attorney.

Along the way other nurses have been curious about what I've accomplished, and I tell them that

Vickie is an awesome woman and she's really worked hard to get where she is. Yet she's actually one of us. She's highly motivating and encouraging.

Vickie Milazzo Institute offers the only program that helps you flourish as a legal nurse consultant. I know one nurse who did a program online, more of a nurse-paralegal program presenting itself as a legal nurse consulting program. She has never done anything with it because she doesn't have the tools to get started.

Every VIP Resource Gives Me New, Easy-to-Use Ideas

I've made good use of the unlimited mentoring with the CLNC® Mentors. They all know me, and the wonderful thing is, no question seems stupid to them. They're so willing to help you succeed. They understand because they've been there, and they give you great ideas on how to get through whatever obstacle or question you're facing.

The other resources of the VIP CLNC® Success System have also been very helpful – they're like my third, fourth and fifth vitals. I frequently refer to Vickie's books; the *Core Curriculum for Legal Nurse Consulting®* textbook, *Flash 55: 55 FREE Ways to Promote Your CLNC® Business* and *Create Your Own Magic for CLNC® Success*, for fresh ideas on how to enhance my business. All of Vickie's books are well written and easy to follow.

I Have a Fresh Attitude Toward Nursing and a Rewarding New Way to Help Patients

The most rewarding thing about my CLNC® business is that I get to continue helping patients and their families. In the course of my business,

> *During the CLNC® Certification Seminar I found myself just waiting for every word that came out of her mouth. Her teaching style is fresh, down to earth and easy to follow.*

I have met with the attorneys' clients, either a surviving patient or the family of a patient who has passed away. I've actually sat with them, held their hands, listened to their traumatic stories and made friends in the process. Then when the case goes to trial, I've seen their reaction when they recover the damages they deserve for the error that occurred – their satisfaction at receiving justice and their relief that the ordeal is finally over. You can't take away the loss they suffered, but knowing that you were able to help them find satisfaction and make the loss more bearable is very rewarding.

Becoming a Certified Legal Nurse Consultant[CM] has changed my life because it's given me a new, fresh attitude toward nursing, the work nurses do, and the incredible reward they experience from making someone better as well as the dissatisfaction they feel when they could have done more if they'd had the time. I've actually learned more nursing than I ever would have learned in the hospital because I'm now dealing with adult disease processes and surgery cases in addition to neonatal and pediatric cases which are my specialty. As a CLNC® consultant I have a renewed sense of where I'm going, what I'm doing and what I'm meant to do, and this profession is a perfect fit for me.

I Gained by Investing in My Future as a Certified Legal Nurse Consultant^{CM}

by Donna du Bois, RNC, MPH, CLNC, Texas

Several of my coworkers took the CLNC® Certification Program and raved about it. All are now Certified Legal Nurse Consultants^{CM} making good money consulting. Two were near retirement and needed additional income to continue their comfortable lifestyles. They are both retired and now earn more than they ever did in their regular jobs.

The program seemed expensive to me, and I decided I didn't need it. Then out of the blue an attorney's office called to ask if I would review some cases. His staff had seen my name on a website and realized from my credentials that I had the long term care expertise they needed. I didn't have a clue what to charge, but the legal nurse consultant hiring me was kind enough to tell me what other consultants charged. I realized I loved working on medical-legal cases, but in order to continue, I needed to know more.

I am certain those two cases would have been my last cases with this attorney if I hadn't enrolled in Vickie's CLNC® Certification Program. He simply would have stopped using me, and I never would have known why.

I purchased the CLNC® Certification Program and took Vickie's valuable advice. I quickly learned the value of contracts. In my excitement at the attorney's call, I accepted two assignments without a contract. I could have put in hours of hard work and never been paid. Vickie's program provided sample contracts I could easily modify for my needs.

Before becoming a Certified Legal Nurse Consultant[CM], I knew I had expertise in one nursing field, but Vickie showed me how to apply my expertise to a multitude of different types of cases. I would never have had the confidence to diversify or even thought to attempt it without her training.

The CLNC® Certification Program is so comprehensive, it's worth years of college education. I was never too tired to listen because Vickie's presentation makes the information interesting and relevant to my needs. The CLNC® Certification Program gave me all the tools I need to succeed as a CLNC® consultant. The sections on marketing, business development and report writing are worth the cost, not to mention the legal background essential for legal nurse consulting. I have never had a course with more useful information. Nothing is left to chance.

I am now confident in my ability to succeed as a full-time, self-employed CLNC® consultant. For now, I prefer to keep my job and consult part time. I plan to retire from nursing home investigation in five years. Thanks to Vickie's program, I know how to market, and I'll have a significant client base established by the time I choose to retire.

Anyone taking the CLNC® Certification Program can quickly earn back its cost many times over, even working only a few extra hours a month. I did. I recommend taking the program *before* you start consulting to avoid making mistakes that could cost you money, clients and your reputation.

As my coworkers tried to tell me, the CLNC® Certification Program is an investment in my future, not an expense. I'm so excited about my success I want to share my enthusiasm.

The CLNC®
Certification
Program
is so
comprehensive,
it's worth
years of
college
education.

Vickie's Simple Networking Tips for Legal Nurse Consultants Paid Off Fast

by Sandra Broad, RN, CLNC, Florida

I can't believe it! Just three weeks after I completed Vickie's CLNC® Certification Seminar, I'm off and running.

I want everyone to know that referrals and networking really do pay off. I followed Vickie's simple tips about networking and marketing, and I'm amazed at how quick and easy it was. I asked a friend if she knew any attorneys in the area, she gave me a name. I went to see him and explained my CLNC® services.

Three days later he called to see if I would be interested in reviewing up to 200 cases a month from various emergency departments across the country for alleged medical injuries and billing inaccuracy. I jumped at the chance! What a great opportunity for my first job as a Certified Legal Nurse Consultant[CM].

I couldn't have done it without Vickie's marketing techniques and wonderful advice. Her CLNC® Certification Program truly is making *all* my dreams come true. A most heartfelt thank you to Vickie and her staff.

I followed Vickie's simple tips about networking and marketing, and I'm amazed at how quick and easy it was.

Vickie's CLNC® Certification Program truly is making all my dreams come true.

The CLNC® Certification Seminar Made My Dream of Owning a Legal Nurse Business a Reality

by Michele R. Groff, PHN, MSN, CLNC, California

Owning my own business had always been a goal of mine, although I did not know what shape would finally emerge. My experience in clinical nursing spans over 25 years, from Medicare hospices to home healthcare. In my last position as a director of home health and outpatient nursing services for a hospital system, I was exposed to medical records review and realized I could reach my goal as a Certified Legal Nurse Consultant℠.

I looked at the different programs available and even checked into several university programs, which were all paralegal-based. Then luckily, I saw an ad for Vickie's CLNC® Certification Program, which emphasized using my nursing experience and applying it to the field of law. This seemed to be a perfect fit for me. Since nursing has given me so much, I strongly agree with Vickie's perspective. As an advocate for RNs, she warns us not to fall into the role of paralegal.

I enrolled in the CLNC® Certification Seminar and felt immediately connected. Anyone starting

I strongly agree with Vickie. As an advocate for RNs, she warns us not to fall into the role of paralegal.

Anyone starting legal nurse consulting needs Vickie's guidance, business savvy and valuable marketing tips.

out in the field of legal nurse consulting needs Vickie's guidance, business savvy and valuable marketing tips. Vickie's CLNC® Mentoring Program has been critical to my success as a beginning CLNC® consultant. Purchasing all of Vickie's educational materials has also helped get my practice off the ground. I've used each and every one.

Vickie inspired me so much that I immediately quit my full-time position and started my own consulting practice. As an independent CLNC® consultant, I get to work on a variety of cases, and I also get to work as a testifying expert. I especially love the medical malpractice cases. Right now, I have 13 cases, and they all came to me by word of mouth.

Referrals Multiplied Our Legal Nurse Consulting Business Fast

*by Sharon Moser, RN, CLNC and
Kathy Thompson, RN, CLNC, Ohio*

After attending the CLNC® Certification Seminar, we told a physician friend what we had just accomplished. She immediately suggested contacting her husband, an attorney. The week after Vickie's program we had our first interview and left his office with two cases. Each time we turn in one case, we get another, sometimes two. The first attorney we worked with introduced us to another attorney, and we are now consulting on the biggest case that firm has ever had. We were able to quit our full-time positions at the hospital and continue nursing part-time in just three months.

We have been so fortunate. The word-of-mouth referrals just keep coming in. We now work closely with three different attorneys. Each one has remarked how well prepared we are and what a good job we do. Just last week we received eight referrals because our clients want their colleagues to know about Certified Legal Nurse Consultants^CM. "Attorneys really don't know about the medical issues in their cases," our attorney-clients say.

We have weekly meetings with attorneys from one firm to keep them updated on all the cases we are working on for them. The attorneys listen to us and value our opinions. It feels great!

We were able to quit our full-time positions at the hospital and continue nursing part-time in just three months.

We are our own bosses, and we learn something new every day.

Our cases are keeping us very busy, and we still have time to enjoy our lives. Most important, we are doing a job we feel proud of while helping others. We are our own bosses, and we learn something new every day. Vickie's CLNC® Certification Program was the step we needed to push us where we wanted to go. We should have done it years ago.

We believe our success so far is directly related to the CLNC® Certification Program. Vickie taught us the little things we would never have known, such as how to approach an attorney and how to market our services. She even includes sample letters to attorneys which we used successfully. Other programs were available to us, but we chose Vickie's because she taught each of us everything needed to succeed.

The CLNC®
Certification
Guaranteed My
First Case

by Martha Bishop,
RN, CLNC, Tennessee

'RNs earn
up to $150/
hr.' Who
could pass
up an
opportunity
like this?"

The week
of Vickie's
seminar
was
amazing."

RNs earn up to $150/hr." Who could pass up an opportunity like this? To a staff nurse earning less than $20/hr, this sounded intriguing, so I opened the large white envelope from Vickie Milazzo Institute and read on. I must have read the contents of that envelope four or five times.

Then I called some attorneys in my area and asked them if they were aware of Certified Legal Nurse Consultants^CM and the services they offer. Most were very enthusiastic when they learned of my interest in this career.

One of the attorneys, Mr. Brown, said that he would love to speak with me and asked when I could meet with him. This certainly was not what I expected to hear. I made an appointment, thanked him for his time and hung up. *Wow!* Now what?

My next thought was clothes. What on earth was I going to wear? My wardrobe consisted of jeans, T-shirts, scrubs and a few casual dresses. I called my best friend Marcie, a CPA, and told her what had happened. She graciously offered to loan me a business suit.

With the clothing issue resolved, I focused on the upcoming meeting. When the day finally arrived, I was nervously pumped and ready. I left my house an hour early to avoid being late. When Marcie called to inform me of a motor vehicle crash on the highway, I took an alternate route. So did everyone else. Then there was a wreck on the alternate route. I took a second alternate route, as did others. Despite all my efforts, I arrived ten minutes late for my meeting with Mr. Brown. What a way to make a first impression. Fortunately, he had heard of the traffic situation and understood.

Our meeting lasted almost 40 minutes. He asked about the legal nurse consulting program I planned to attend, and I told him I'd be taking Vickie Milazzo Institute's CLNC® Certification Seminar in a couple of months. I explained that I wanted to help patients in a different venue (and the money sounded good too). He told me to come back to see him after I completed the Institute's CLNC® Certification Program and he would assign me a couple of cases and see what I did with them. *Wow*, again! I had cases waiting and hadn't even taken the CLNC® training yet.

The week of Vickie's seminar was amazing. After learning that I had passed the CLNC® Certification Exam, I called Mr. Brown as promised. We met again. Then he asked about my fees. Nervously, yet confidently, I replied, "$125 an hour." He said, "Okay," and handed me a case. On the way to my van, I thought, "*Wow*! I can do this; I can do anything!"

I screened the case for my new attorney-client. When I finished, I returned the medical record, along with my findings. I mailed him an invoice for my CLNC® services; a few weeks later, he mailed a check.

To celebrate my first case, Marcie and I spent four glorious days in Orlando, riding roller coasters (my husband doesn't ride them). I love roller coasters, the bigger and faster the better.

I have sat at the bedside of a patient dying of cancer. I have played "peek-a-boo" with a sick child in the hospital. I have held a patient's hand during a painful procedure. Now, I have helped a patient who had a meritorious legal case. As Vickie says, "I am a nurse and *I can do anything*!"

I replied, '$125 an hour.' He said, 'Okay,' and handed me a case. I thought, 'Wow! I can do this.'

Developing My Expertise as a Certified Legal Nurse Consultant^{CM} Is the Key to Growing a CLNC® Business

by Erika Aguirre, RN, BSN, MSN, CLNC, Texas

> *Like Vickie teaches, I actually saved the law firm quite a lot of money.*

> *As I presented my report the attorney was visibly impressed.*

G oing into my first case, with Vickie Milazzo Institute's CLNC® Certification Program training fresh in my mind, I was fairly confident. Thirteen years of nursing practice gives an RN plenty of self-assurance around doctors, so I thought I'd do fine with attorneys. And everything did go fine even when I had to tell an attorney his case was not meritorious.

Soon after earning my CLNC® certification, I received a case from an attorney to screen for merit. We studied screening medical-related cases during the CLNC® Certification Seminar, and this wasn't my first case, so I knew exactly what to look for in the medical records. I searched and searched, then turned back to the beginning and searched again. My conclusion – the case was not meritorious.

The attorney had paid a nice retainer and had put his faith in me. How would he feel when I presented my opinion of, "Sorry, no merit"? I studied the medical records again, but this time to support my opinion. I also discussed the case with a seasoned CLNC® Mentor to boost my confidence and get a new perspective on how to approach communicating my opinion to the attorney.

I wrote a three-page report on why the case was defensible. Knowing that these were trial attorneys accustomed to asking probing questions, I wanted all my ducks in a row. Finally, I was ready – I could defend my opinion that this case was not meritorious.

Nervous, even with the facts and proof right in front of me, I made the call. "Keep it clear and concise," I told myself. Using the Vickie Milazzo Institute Case Screening Form to stay focused, I presented my findings.

When I finished the attorney said, "That's wonderful. Thank you." I nearly fell off my chair. Having stressed so much over this upcoming dialogue, I couldn't quite believe what I was hearing – he was okay with a nonmeritorious case.

Like Vickie teaches, I actually saved the law firm quite a lot of money. Going to court and losing a case is costly, often in six-figure amounts. Because of my thorough screening the law firm knew not to pursue this case. The attorney was so completely satisfied and so accepting of my opinion that he affirmed my confidence in myself and my work product. I'd done a good job.

Nothing Beats Confidence to Impress Attorneys as a Certified Legal Nurse Consultant^{CM}

Receiving such a positive response on a nonmeritorious case, especially when I was so

> *Every time the attorneys ask for something new, my training with Vickie Milazzo Institute is right there to guide me – it works.*

nervous going in, was an excellent experience to have early on. It has made me far more comfortable approaching new attorney-prospects.

My second case was meritorious and as I wrote the report, Vickie's voice was right there with me, reminding me that I was presenting myself not as a legal expert, but as a nursing expert. Attorneys need my perspective, and nursing is what I know. We're equals in our different professional expertise. My confidence must have shone through as I presented my report because the attorney was visibly impressed.

After my attorney-client filed a petition he contacted me to provide additional substance and analysis. I was elated. Several months later I continue to be involved in the case working alongside the attorneys. I'm comfortable consulting on this case, seeing it grow and develop, seeing the attorneys take what I've presented and use it to solidify their lawsuit. Every time they ask for something new, my training with Vickie Milazzo Institute is right there to guide me – it works.

The *Core Curriculum for Legal Nurse Consulting®* Textbook, Vickie and the CLNC® Mentors Are Always There for Me

Still new at this, my approach is to stay positive and receptive of everything I'm requested to do. I refer to the *Core Curriculum for Legal Nurse Consulting®* textbook as I research and present whatever the attorney needs. My goal is to always provide the best. Not that I don't get nervous at times, but reminding myself that attorneys are people just like me, and need what I can provide, helps me work through nervousness and focus on the case.

So far, the CLNC® services I've been contracted for include screening for merit, writing reports and locating testifying experts. It's so rewarding to see each part play out and have the attorney come back to me for more.

Nurses don't go to school to learn business and marketing skills, so the challenge of having to sell myself to attorneys was a change for me. Each time an attorney listens to my sales presentation and responds by hiring me as a CLNC® consultant, I get a thrill. I'm loving it. I've had only positive experiences with attorneys and I love that they respect my opinion. Knowing that everyone at Vickie Milazzo Institute has my back and is there to mentor me, provides the confidence to always say, "Yes, I can do that for you."

> *Everyone at Vickie Milazzo Institute has my back and is there to mentor me.*

Vickie Gives You the Tools – You Just Have to Do What She Says

Deep down, when you're considering a career change – putting forth the time, expense and effort – there's a certain level of concern. Is this going to work? I wouldn't want to speak for every beginner legal nurse consultant, but I believe that developing my expertise with each new attorney, each new case and even with each potential failure is the key to growing a sound and profitable CLNC® business.

What would I say to anyone newer than I am? Just this: Get the most out of the CLNC® Certification Program, whether you take it Online or attend a Live seminar. Drink in as much as you can. Do what Vickie instructs you to do – one thing every day. You won't have successes every day, but over time you will build your CLNC® business.

Vickie's CLNC® Certification Program gives you all the tools you need to succeed as a Certified Legal Nurse Consultant^CM. You just have to execute them.

My Recent Exhibiting Experience – What a Win!

by Michelle Wilson,
RN, SANE, CLNC, Oklahoma

I recently exhibited with a CLNC® Mentor at a legal conference in Indianapolis. What a win! The entire experience was so organized from beginning to end, including the call from Vickie Milazzo Institute providing the info I needed to exhibit effectively, and the follow-up reminders from the Institute after exhibiting. The organization and support from the Institute has made the whole process of exhibiting easy and fun, which are two things that I didn't expect on my first big public outing as a Certified Legal Nurse Consultant^CM.

The booth sponsored by the *National Alliance of Certified Legal Nurse Consultants* (*NACLNC®*) was the most lively booth at the legal conference. I learned the value of having an interactive game to both draw the attorneys to the booth and to start a relaxed, easy conversation with them about my legal nurse consulting services and, most important, about the attorneys' needs. The coaching that the CLNC® Mentor gave me ensured that no opportunity for a conversation with an attorney-prospect was missed. I was nervous and awkward at the beginning, but the CLNC® Mentor was so

> *"Attorneys gladly exchanged business cards and talked to me about the legal nurse consulting services I provide."*

supportive that I soon relaxed and "got my USP on."

Attorneys were drawn to the *NACLNC*® exhibit booth by our energy and the interest that we projected. They were happy to spin for free CLNC® services and other prizes. Everyone loves alcohol, candy and something for free! In return they gladly exchanged business cards and talked to me about the legal nurse consulting services I provide.

I went to a follow-up cocktail party and spoke to a couple of the attorneys I had met earlier in the day. I almost didn't go because I was tired, but the CLNC® Mentor explained that informal networking was invaluable.

I returned from exhibiting late Thursday night and Friday I sorted through all my leads, putting them into three categories:

1. Attorneys who won free CLNC® services.

2. Attorneys who won other prizes – e.g. alcohol.

3. People who were not attorneys but might be able to refer me to an attorney in the future.

Then I researched each law firm on the Internet, printed out the attorney's bio and significant information about the legal practice. While researching I looked for some kind of connection that I could mention during my follow-up marketing.

I then sent an email to each person in groups 1 and 2 and spoke to someone in their practice by the end of the day on Friday. By Saturday

> *I heard from an attorney I met at the cocktail party, who had just sent four cases to my Dropbox!*

> *I discussed my fee (he didn't even hesitate).*

night, I had my first response from an attorney taking advantage of his free CLNC® service. By Monday morning I heard from a second attorney I met at the cocktail party, who had just sent four cases to my Dropbox! Even though I had to work several 12-hour shifts that week, I spoke with him, discussed my fee (he didn't even hesitate) and sent and received my contract back. I'm off to an amazing start and have since heard from another attorney requesting more information.

I live in St. Louis so I'm consulting long distance with these attorneys and it's working beautifully. I will be following up monthly with all the leads through a blog or newsletter and plan to start working my local attorney base. I'm also planning my 2015 exhibiting schedule in Missouri, Minnesota and Indianapolis. My goal is to exhibit at least three times in 2015 and to pursue other networking opportunities locally. I'm going on my honeymoon to Hawaii in January, and you can be sure I will be sending packets out ahead and setting up attorney interviews while there.

The best thing about exhibiting as a Certified Legal Nurse Consultant℠ was the confidence it gave me and the clarity of direction. I am positive that I can make this my new full-time job. But I'll still joyfully work a shift in the ED once in a while just because I love the patients.

Thanks for this exhibiting opportunity – and special thanks to the Vickie Milazzo Institute staff and the CLNC® Mentors. Mentoring is the icing on this CLNC® cake!

I'm consulting long distance and it's working beautifully.

Mentoring is the icing on this CLNC® cake!

Legal Nurse Consulting Rejuvenated My Relationship with Nursing

by Cynthia S. Bune, RN, CLNC, Wisconsin

I suddenly realized the love affair I had with the nursing job that I held so dear to me had come to an end. The differences were dividing our relationship between personal values and corporate goals. I knew that I was growing and had to move on.

One of my favorite things to do as an RN was to dig in the charts of my complex patients. I found myself time and time again presenting information that many of the other healthcare professionals had no idea even existed.

I had been interested in legal nurse consulting for some time. I'd received information on Vickie Milazzo Institute's CLNC® Certification Program years before. As so many of us have done, I did not "see the forest for the trees," I just kept on working as I was the sole breadwinner for my family of five. The subject of what I was going to do for myself came to mind constantly. Much to my dismay I realized I was losing a grip on my nursing career. I only had one thought of what I wanted to do next. I wanted to become a Certified Legal Nurse ConsultantᶜᴹCM.

I told myself that I was going to research the subject for at least six weeks. After a few weeks of being on the phone with dozens of people, it became very clear; those who took Vickie's CLNC® Certification Program and did what she taught found success! Those who took other courses simply were not successful. I was sold.

I became certified by the end of April. My instincts were correct. The CLNC® Certification Seminar was fabulous. Vickie Milazzo shares everything; she holds nothing back. As time went on, I learned that everything Vickie taught was always right on target.

I was consumed with taking an action step every day and I found myself working full time to launch my legal nurse consulting business. I knew that I was taking a chance. Vickie had even stated that she did not suggest we run out and quit our jobs. She actually recommended starting part time as a Certified Legal Nurse Consultant℠, especially if our family's income came from our nursing jobs. I could tell she just wanted us to be careful and not act haphazardly. I felt her confidence in what she was teaching, and as a friend to nursing, I knew that she wanted us to make mindful choices.

Everything was falling into place for me. The timing, the support from my family and the best part – my excitement regarding my nursing career was rejuvenated again.

I decided to invest by exhibiting at a legal conference. My first exhibiting experience was a

Vickie shares everything; she holds nothing back.

As time went on, I learned that everything Vickie taught was always right on target.

This attorney said that my work was terrific, 'second to none.'

positive one. I had not done so well at the 2-Day *NACLNC®* Apprenticeship when we practiced interviewing with attorneys. At the Apprenticeship, I had an opportunity to be up in front of everybody and was very nervous. I decided that I could not afford to be outwardly nervous with attorneys. If I wanted to be a professional, I must present like one. From phone calls to letters to exhibiting at legal conferences, I found that it was really no different than speaking to all of the intellects that I had dealt with throughout my nursing career.

My first case was a free case screening that an attorney won at my exhibit. He actually put two cards in the drawing. The case spanned a period of more than four and a half years. I agreed to write a brief report. I summarized this case identifying its weaknesses and strengths in three pages. I then followed up with my recommendations. I still carry with me and cannot erase the voicemail that this attorney left on my phone. He was so thrilled with my work that he told me he wanted to work with me on other cases. He said that my work was terrific, "second to none." I was absolutely thrilled. The next day (after he had called me) I received two more calls from attorneys who wanted to discuss my CLNC® services. Both of these attorneys have since hired me. I was confident in the meetings and the attorneys said they liked what they heard and were impressed by my work product.

Here's the ironic part: While meeting for my first paid job, I stated that I required a retainer before starting the work. The attorney immediately asked his assistant to cut me a check. When his assistant came in and asked me for my tax ID number, I immediately turned into a babbling fool. I had forgotten my tax ID number that I had previously memorized. My heart was pounding and I was starting to sweat. I wanted to tear up or maybe even pass out. Why was I suddenly so nervous? Oh my gosh it was finally happening – I was not nervous – I was overcome with excitement! I was really a Certified Legal Nurse Consultant^{CM}!

"I received two more calls. Both of these attorneys have since hired me."

Triumph Over Any Personal Challenge

Shoulder Injuries Killed My Nursing Career – Vickie Milazzo Brought It Back to Life

by Cheryl L. Bennett,
RN, BSN, CLNC, Indiana

I'm a combat veteran – part of the Grenada invasion – with 30 years in nursing. You'd think I'd be immune to on-the-job injuries.

After leaving the military, I finished my federal career at the Department of Veterans' Affairs. I was also working PRN at a psych hospital. One night three patients assaulted me and injured my right shoulder. When that had almost healed, I returned to work at the VA hospital. In no way was I playing Super Nurse, as I'm prone to do, but while helping six other people lift a patient, I injured my left shoulder.

In only a year I've just about replaced my nursing salary – and I earned a very good salary.

That second injury killed my nursing career as I knew it. Workers' comp settled for far less than I expected, even though I got the maximum amount. The only way to get my life back was to invest that money in myself and in a new future.

Over the years I had seen Vickie Milazzo Institute's advertisement in nursing journals and thought that someday I might like to become a Certified Legal Nurse Consultant[CM]. My shoulder injury made "someday" come sooner than I expected.

One Magic Pen Later – A Referral Kicked Off My CLNC® Career

Five months after attending the CLNC® Certification Seminar, I received a promotional ballpoint pen – bright colors, my name, address and phone number printed on the side. It struck me that this was the only evidence of my being in business. I didn't even have business cards yet. I stuffed the pen in my purse.

A few days later I ran into a nurse I hadn't seen for quite a while. We chatted, and I told her about my new "career" as a Certified Legal Nurse Consultant[CM]. Embarrassed that I didn't have a business card, I gave her the pen. "Here's my phone number," I said. "We can get together and have lunch."

About two months after I gave away the "magic" pen, I got a call from a law firm. The attorney said, "You come highly recommended."

The only way to get my life back was to invest that money in myself and in a new future.

I got a call from a law firm. The attorney said, 'You come highly recommended.'

Highly recommended? I hadn't done a case yet. I asked if I could call back. I panicked about what to say.

"What Would Vickie Do Now?" Inspired Me to Action

Frantically, I pulled out the *Core Curriculum for Legal Nurse Consulting®* textbook, thinking, "What would Vickie do now?" Everything I needed was in that book.

Vickie said to always get a retainer. When I called the attorney back, I told him the hourly rate and that I required a $500 retainer before taking the case. He said, "No problem." At this point I still didn't know where he had gotten my name.

When I arrived at the attorney's office, the check was waiting. The attorney said, "I need you to locate an expert witness." I expected him to say he needed a nurse experienced in nursing home care, critical care or emergency. Instead, he said, "This is an excessive force case against the police department. I need someone trained in how to control people who are combative."

Was he serious? Yes. And he needed this person in 48 hours. "I can do it," I said, without a clue how I would manage.

He didn't seem at all worried. "The nurse who gave me your name said you can do anything."

Now I finally knew who had referred me, the nurse I'd given the pen to, the nurse I'd run into totally by accident. That proved to me what I'd

Everything I needed was in the Core Curriculum for Legal Nurse Consulting® *textbook.*

I told him the hourly rate and that I required a $500 retainer. He said, 'No problem.'

learned in Vickie's seminar, that people know attorneys. All you have to do is tell enough people what you're doing and ask them to pass your name along.

I remembered that my sister-in-law has a degree in criminal justice. I called her. She said, "What you want is a certified instructor in defense tactics for disturbed behavior." She even knew a couple of people who qualified.

Then I remembered a nurse from the VA hospital. Her husband is a police officer who is certified and has won awards in using a baton to subdue. I called him and he agreed to be a witness.

Within 24 hours I had not one but three expert witnesses to fulfill my commitment to the attorney. He was so impressed, his response was, "I want you on my team."

Four Attorneys Keep Me Busy

Walking through my attorney-client's building, I recognized other attorneys. I'd seen them on the news being interviewed about their high-profile cases. One of these attorneys stopped by my client's office while I was there. Two days later, she called me. She had intended to use a nurse she knew on a case, but after hearing about me, had decided I was the better choice. I ended up with a big case on nursing home abuse.

Now the word is out. Every time I turn around, someone says, "We hear you do such a good job. When can you consult with us?"

I work with four attorneys, and that's keeping me busy. I can handle that many by managing my time well. In only a year I've just about replaced my nursing salary – and I earned a *very* good salary.

I'm amazed that I was so afraid of getting started. Vickie tells us exactly what to do – and it works. When I bumped into my friend and gave her that promotional pen with my phone number, without thinking I was following Vickie's advice, "Just do it." The nurse passed my name along with a terrific recommendation, and my career as a Certified Legal Nurse Consultant^{CM} snowballed.

None of this would have happened without the CLNC® training. When I was at the CLNC® Certification Seminar, still suffering with chronic shoulder pain, Vickie's positive message came through loud and clear. Even with my traditional nursing career dead, I didn't have to sit at home moaning, "Poor me. My life is over." I owe my new life to Vickie, not only to her excellent training but also to the inspiration that comes from just being around her.

> *I owe my new life to Vickie, not only to her excellent training but also to the inspiration that comes from just being around her.*

I Earned $138,000 in Less Than 18 Months as a Certified Legal Nurse Consultant^{CM}

*by Kathy G. Ferrell,
RN, BSN, CLNC, Alabama*

For ten years I was a nurse manager with a corporation to which I was dedicated. Then upper management changed, and the atmosphere became unbearable. My family and friends urged me to get out, but fear of change paralyzed me. My best friend had attended Vickie Milazzo's CLNC® Certification Seminar, and she knew legal nurse consulting would fit me perfectly. For a year she urged me to attend – still I was too afraid to make the change.

In my position as nurse manager, I worked with the legal department regularly. I finally decided that knowing something about legal nurse consulting would benefit me in my current career, and I signed up for the CLNC® Certification Seminar.

Vickie Opened a New Window for Me

Then without warning, I received an offer I could not refuse – resign or be terminated. In 28 years as a registered nurse, I had never experienced such a devastating blow. My heart hurt, my pride was wounded and my self-confidence all but died.

I felt like I was crawling on the floor, struggling to find the strength to climb out a window. My salvation was that I had already registered for the CLNC® Certification Seminar.

At the seminar one of the first things out of Vickie's mouth was, "We are nurses and we can do anything!®" How refreshing to hear that I was capable of doing anything. Vickie's enthusiasm was uplifting and contagious. Best of all, she was sincere. She had succeeded as a nurse and as a legal nurse consultant herself and had mentored many other nurses to CLNC® success.

In addition to Vickie's assurance that I could do it, I heard from other nurses who had met the challenge, succeeded and were willing to help me succeed. The CLNC® Certification Program was excellent and was presented in a way that kept me interested and even entertained. I had fun. I became determined to show Vickie and especially myself that I could be a successful Certified Legal Nurse Consultant^{CM}. Sure enough, a new window was opened for me.

Vickie's Action Steps Are the Key to Freedom, Flexibility and Success

How did I do it? I went home, and every day I took one of Vickie's action steps toward my new career as a Certified Legal Nurse Consultant^{CM}. I mailed my information packets and within a week I began calling for appointments. I bucked up my courage to keep knocking on those doors, because I

> *Vickie's enthusiasm was uplifting and contagious. Best of all, she was sincere. She had mentored many other nurses to CLNC® success.*

was convinced I had knowledge and experience that could benefit the attorneys.

Several of those initial contacts eventually became clients. One attorney called me back after receiving my packet and said, "I need help. I'm drowning!" Just four months after I became a CLNC® consultant, I received my first four cases from him and made a good friend in the process.

In my first year as a CLNC® consultant I made more than $68,000 from eight very respectable attorney-clients. In the next six months. I made another $70,000.

Best of all I have the flexibility to spend more time with my husband (and business manager), my children and my hobbies. The freedom that being a Certified Legal Nurse Consultant^CM affords is unsurpassed. I offer my sincere thanks to Vickie and all the dedicated staff at Vickie Milazzo Institute for helping me become a successful CLNC® consultant. I am a nurse and I can do anything!

One attorney called me back and said, 'I need help. I'm drowning!' Just four months after I became a CLNC® consultant, I received my first four cases from him.

How I Survived Downsizing and Divorce to Triumph as a CLNC® Consultant

by Dale Barnes, RN, MSN, PHN, CLNC, California

Seven years ago, I was director of home care, home infusion, hospice and lifeline emergency services at a well-known hospital – a prestigious job with excellent salary and benefits. The work was challenging and fun, and I really enjoyed my coworkers, both administrative colleagues and my staff. I had built a cohesive team, doubled my department's revenues, decreased costs and implemented many new systems. I was proud of becoming a businesswoman while remaining a nurse, and I was on a "high."

However, the hospital hired a new CEO who had very different plans. My job was eliminated, and they hired a businesswoman to run the department. She had no idea about the staff's nursing and clinical needs. Two years later, they realized their mistake and hired a clinical person for the position.

Meanwhile, I found a similar job as head of a hospital department for all home-care-related services. This job presented two major challenges: the department had no computer system and the employees were unionized. Just as things began coming together, the hospital was sold to a large

> *My first case came from a friend who practices estate law. This case brought more referrals.*

I got a call from an attorney who desperately needed the services of a CLNC® consultant. I was in his office within two hours and walked out with a personal injury case. This attorney became a good client and gave my name to several colleagues.

corporation. Within two months, my department was closed, and all employees received severance packages and were sent on their way.

I was the victim of downsizing yet again. As if these career catastrophes weren't enough, four-and-a-half years ago, I got divorced for the second time.

What was I to do? Here I was, divorced, jobless and not wanting to go through another downsizing episode. My severance package would not last forever, and being dependant on my ex-husband did not appeal to me.

For a long time I had been receiving information about Vickie's CLNC® Certification Program. It sounded interesting, but I hadn't had time to pursue it. Now I pulled out one of those flyers, called for more information – and felt I had found my answer.

Determination Paved the Way to Certification

Many years ago, I owned my own home-care agencies. I liked being my own boss. I had good business sense and people skills, and I enjoyed a challenge. My background was in oncology, then home health and hospice. I had my master's in psych and had worked in that arena for a while. I knew such an eclectic background would serve me well as a Certified Legal Nurse Consultant℠, but I needed to earn money while building my CLNC® business.

I called on a friend in the home health field, the nursing director of a home infusion company. He said he needed another field nurse, and I jumped at the chance, knowing that as a per diem employee I would have a lot of flexibility. I loved working with the patients and could work as little or as much as I chose.

I ordered Vickie's CLNC® Certification Program. I watched portions of the program almost every day. I was sure I'd be able to finish the course, study and take the exam in six months. But life has a funny way of throwing us curve balls.

On my 50th birthday, I boasted that I did not feel 50. Nine years earlier I had an inoperable, nonmalignant brain tumor. I had an annual MRI to ensure the tumor had not moved or grown, and I felt well and healthy. But two weeks after my 50th birthday I got very sick. I had some strange auto-immune symptoms and was left with no hearing in my right ear and unsteady balance. I was told that the 8th cranial nerve had been permanently destroyed, but that the problem was unrelated to my brain lesion. I was unable to ascertain from which direction sound was coming. That problem remains with me, but I have learned to compensate.

The most annoying and frustrating result was that I couldn't study the CLNC® Certification Program for a few months. I felt a sense of urgency about completing the necessary work. Finally, I finished the program and passed the CLNC® Certification Exam.

"A couple of my best attorney-clients said they wanted to use me on every medical-related case. Using my expertise was more cost-effective than doing it themselves."

I Contacted Attorneys Every Day

I was anxious to get started and decided to be a little aggressive. First, I contacted attorneys I knew, regardless of their specialty, and asked for referrals. My attorney friends were intrigued by what I was doing.

I made phone calls every day. I put together a packet of information to send to new contacts. My first case came from a friend who practices estate law. She had me go with her to a hospital to help assess a terminal patient so she could write a bedside will. I addressed the client's competency to make decisions based on physical condition, mental status and any medication effects. This case brought more referrals from the estate attorney.

Another friend who practices labor law had no work for me himself, but passed out my flyers at a meeting of plaintiff attorneys. The next morning, I got a call from an attorney who had picked up a flyer. He desperately needed the services of a CLNC® consultant and asked how soon I could come to see him. I was in his office within two hours and walked out with a personal injury case related to a motor vehicle accident. This attorney became a good client and gave my name to several colleagues.

Interestingly enough, my attorney-clients had either plodded through the medical records or hired physicians. Many of them wanted to know why I thought I could do a better job than they could. They believed that because they had been doing it for so many years themselves, they really understood the medical issues. Fortunately, I was able to show them that they did need me, and that using my expertise was more cost-effective than doing it themselves. A couple of my best attorney-clients said they wanted to use me on every medical-related case. This was a good break for me, but unfortunately, these clients were not getting dozens of such cases every week. So I continued to work my day job.

My Marketing Efforts Paid Off Big

I joined three different networking groups and attended meetings religiously. After a while other members get to know you, understand what you do and become confident in giving you referrals. Most referrals from these groups came not from the attorneys in the group, but from attorneys other members knew and had me contact. I also started sending out an information newsletter every other month.

My efforts started paying off. Before I knew it, attorneys I did not know or contact were calling me. Attorneys for whom I worked were giving my name to other attorneys. I also gained three steady clients from my newsletters, a good response given that my mailing was only going to about 400 attorneys at the time.

One of these steady clients is an attorney who specializes in dog bites and manages cases from coast to coast. I get 10-12 of these cases per month, from simple cases to those involving disfiguring

One steady client specializes in dog bites. This client provides me with steady income every single month, and the work is the easiest I do.

injuries. I summarize the medical records for each case and provide the attorney a 1-2 page overview describing the injuries, treatment and possible future treatment. I charge for my time tracking and reviewing the cases and writing the reports. This client provides me with steady income every single month, and the work is the easiest I do. I have other steady clients, but their assignments are more complex. The combination is exciting and challenging.

Referrals Kept My CLNC® Business Flowing

Last year I moved from Los Angeles to San Diego. About six months before the move, I asked an attorney friend in L.A. if he knew any San Diego attorneys. He came up with several association lists of both plaintiff and defense attorneys. I made numerous phone calls and set up appointments with as many of these potential clients as I could. I always used my friend's name, stating that he had referred me and given me their number. Although he only knew a few of them personally, no one came right out and said they never heard of him.

From these contacts came a multitude of new clients. One attorney actually handed me medical records as I left his office after our first meeting. Another attorney asked me to speak to his firm about the CLNC® services I could provide on bad faith insurance cases. Another contact referred me to his buddy in the San Diego city attorney's office, who became a client.

From these contacts came a multitude of new clients. One attorney actually handed me medical records as I left his office after our first meeting.

Sometimes I am so overwhelmed with work that I subcontract with other CLNC® consultants.

Word of mouth was again a plus for me. After I had lived in San Diego for only three weeks, 40% of my client base was here. Referrals have helped my San Diego clientele grow. I have already received inquiries and requests for my CLNC® services from attorneys who heard about me through other attorneys. I stressed to my Los Angeles clients (still 60% of my client base) that their cases will continue to receive the same quality service as when I lived in L.A. Email and FedEx® are wonderful.

I Made the Leap Into a Full-Time CLNC® Business

Despite these successes, until recently I continued to see home health patients for two agencies to earn "bread and butter" money. I always knew I could supplement my income with home health visits if the phone stopped ringing for a few days. In addition, my home health work gave me the clinical continuity to feel comfortable testifying about clinical issues.

At one of the *NACLNC®* Conferences, Vickie talked about taking that leap and letting go of secondary work in order to build your CLNC® practice into a full-time business. I really wanted to do this, but it was scary. After that conference I went home and told both home health agencies to call me only if they were really desperate for a nurse. Slowly, I weaned myself away and was able to tell them to take me off their rosters.

What my CLNC® practice has brought me is total freedom. I feel emancipated. I no longer need the home health income; I have more than surpassed that.

*I love
what I
am doing.
I'm busy,
challenged
and
financially
secure. I've
overcome
downsizing
and divorce
to achieve
more than
I ever felt
possible.*

When attorneys ask about testifying, I tell them I will find a clinically active nurse to testify. I explain that although I still testify to the findings of medical record reviews, I no longer testify to clinical issues. This too was a leap, as my rate for testifying is double my consulting rate. I felt like I was letting go of a lifeline, but I reminded myself that testifying to clinical issues was not the bulk of my business. Then I took the plunge anyway.

Sometimes I am so overwhelmed with work that I cannot complete it all in a timely manner. I then subcontract with other CLNC® consultants.

What my CLNC® business has brought me is total freedom. I feel emancipated. I no longer need the home health visit income; I have more than surpassed that. I don't have any desire to go back to a clinical setting. At times I do miss the patient contact, but I often get quite involved with the attorneys' clients. Many of them call me to ask for medical resources or nursing advice.

I feel like I have the best of all worlds. I am so happy Vickie encouraged me to step out of my comfort zone. I love what I am doing. I'm busy, challenged and financially secure, and I am so proud to be a Certified Legal Nurse Consultant[CM]. I've overcome both downsizing and divorce to achieve more than I ever felt possible.

My CLNC® Career Gave Me a New Life for Myself and My Twins

by Lisa Panish, RN, MSN, ARNP-BC, CLNC, Florida

"I love you one million peanut butter cups. That's a lot of love." My twin boys and I repeat that to each other every night before we go to bed. I know I'm lucky. What do you say about the most important people in your life? My five-year-old identical twins are the reason I became a Certified Legal Nurse Consultant[CM] – both have cerebral palsy and asthma.

I have been a single mom since my sons were 15 months old. As a healthcare provider, I have been blessed with opportunities that many others have not. I've been a nurse practitioner for almost ten years, and I have a wonderful job and colleagues. However, I was missing opportunities and therapies with my children. Sometimes I don't want to blink, because I don't want to miss anything in their lives.

As fulfilled and busy as my life is, my parents encouraged me to challenge myself more and try another opportunity. I learned about becoming a CLNC® consultant from my mother's nursing college roommate, who reported finding success and versatility in her new CLNC® career. Immediately after that conversation, the Vickie

I attended the CLNC® Certification Seminar, and every minute was invaluable. The wealth of information fascinated me.

Within three months I had three attorney-clients.

Milazzo Institute information packet arrived in my mailbox.

My parents and I discussed the opportunity to work from home, enjoy a flexible schedule and use my nursing skills in a different way. My parents are so helpful, but they want to enjoy their retirement. The more we heard about the Vickie Milazzo Institute CLNC® Certification Program, the more we all agreed that the CLNC® Certification Seminar was a good investment.

Within 3 Months of Becoming a CLNC® Consultant, I Had 3 Attorney-Clients

I attended the CLNC® Certification Seminar, and every minute was invaluable. The wealth of information fascinated me, and I knew I had found a nursing profession I could excel in and enjoy.

I returned home full of motivation and ready to get started, but the responsibilities of a full-time job and sick children took priority. My friends knew I had taken Vickie's program and were excited for me. One girlfriend called to tell me that her neighbor, an attorney, was looking for a Certified Legal Nurse Consultant℠ to do some work for him.

And so my CLNC® career began. It all happened so quickly. My first case was the scariest, and I kept thinking, "Fake it till you make it." How many times did I hear that?

After that first case, my CLNC® colleagues began calling me when they were overloaded. I completed

My attorney-clients refer me to their attorney colleagues — last week I received a call from a defense attorney.

two more cases, and within three months I had three attorney-clients. My attorney-clients now refer me to their attorney colleagues – last week I received a call from a defense attorney.

The learning curve has been huge, and the social atmosphere in the legal world is different from that in the hospitals, nursing homes and office practices where I have worked. On every case I am able to give the nursing perspective and add my personal experience as a nurse practitioner to strengthen the case. I look forward to challenging myself with other CLNC® opportunities and becoming more versatile. I want attorneys to see me as an asset and call on me because of my outstanding reputation in my new career.

With the money I have made so far as a CLNC® consultant, I have been able to replace the tile and carpet throughout my home with hardwood floors. This change has made a difference in my boys' asthma and their mobility. I have wanted to change the flooring since I moved in four years ago, but was never able to afford it until I became a CLNC® consultant.

I cannot thank Vickie Milazzo Institute enough for changing not only my life, but the lives of my special boys.

With the money I have made as a CLNC® consultant, I have replaced the carpet throughout my home with hardwood floors. This has made a difference in my boys' asthma and their mobility.

Feel the Beat of CLNC® Success – Then Get Out and Dance!

by Jan Boswell, RN, MSN, CLNC, Alabama

My partner and I have a motivational saying that hangs in both our offices. It defines success as getting out on the dance floor. Joyce and I have been successfully dancing the CLNC® dance for nearly two years. This is the story of our dance, both the upbeats and the downbeats.

I was a single mother of two when I started noticing the ads in nursing journals: "Earn $125-$150/hr." Wow! I called for the Vickie Milazzo Institute information packet, I watched the legal nurse consulting video and I was hooked.

The Freedom of Working from Home Was Music to My Ears

Until my divorce I had stayed home with my children, one of whom has severe learning disabilities. My kids were fast approaching their teenage years. They needed me at home. The possibility of being able to work from home and make good money as a Certified Legal Nurse Consultant^{CM} was music to my ears. Now I had to put my toe onto the dance floor. I admit I was scared.

I worked full-time float at the hospital. Many nights I got pulled to CICU where I worked with Joyce who was also thinking about becoming a

A few weeks after we started our CLNC® business, we received our first big case from one of the legends in the law community. Our CLNC® services made a big contribution to the $12-million verdict our attorney-client won.

CLNC® consultant. We talked about becoming partners – she could dance the CLNC® dance with me.

I ordered the CLNC® Certification Program. Although the material seemed challenging at first, I grew more excited with every module I finished. I took my CLNC® Certification Exam and passed! That was the first upbeat note of my CLNC® dance.

The month after I became a CLNC® consultant, Joyce took the CLNC® Certification Seminar and also passed the CLNC® Exam. Our music was starting to play.

Our First Big Case Got Us Onto the Dance Floor with a $12-Million Verdict

A few weeks after we started our CLNC® business, we received our first big case from one of the legends in the local law community. This helped us overcome all our fears. We had to do it. Our CLNC® services made a big contribution to the $12-million verdict our attorney-client won.

Even though we continued to work full-time at the hospital that first year, we earned $40,000 from our CLNC® business. While the music and the dance were often chaotic, we were having the time of our lives. We never missed a beat of the music. In one week we got eight cases. We just kept working on cases and making money.

> *Even though we continued to work full-time at the hospital, we earned $40,000 from our CLNC® business.*

> *We were having the time of our lives. In one week we got eight cases. We just kept working on cases and making money.*

Our Ever-Changing CLNC® Dance Keeps Our Successful Business Fun

Currently, we have three attorneys who consult with us regularly. We have consulted on medical malpractice, drug product liability and insurance fraud cases working for both plaintiff and defense attorneys. From case to case, the music changes and the dance is different – that's what makes our CLNC® business so much fun.

I work from home and this makes a tremendous difference for me and my children – we love being together.

I work from home and this makes a tremendous difference for me and my children – we love being together.

Joyce and I are both goal oriented. Our goal this year is to double or triple our income. We let nothing stop us. That's what it takes to succeed: persistence, faith and action. It's all about staying on the dance floor and dancing the dance.

Finding My Passion as a CLNC® Consultant Puts a Song in My Heart Every Day

So many people have helped me succeed. Joyce and I keep each other motivated. Of course, I always hear Vickie's voice in my head. The CLNC® Mentors are great, and the success stories of my CLNC® peers inspire me. But the people who help me the most are my kids. They have given up time with me and never complained. They applaud my successes and pull me through my missteps. They are the reason I am dancing the dance. They are the sweetest music in my life.

My CLNC® career has changed me and my life. I see a bright future for myself. The most important change is that I have found my passion. I am happiest when working on a case, calling a client or working on a new marketing strategy. I have a song in my heart all the time.

If you're wondering whether you can make it as a Certified Legal Nurse Consultant^{CM}, just put your toe on the dance floor, listen to the music and dance. You'll have the time of your life. I am!

My CLNC® career has changed me. I have found my passion. You'll have the time of your life. I am!

I Love Going for It as a Certified Legal Nurse Consultant^{CM}

by Jeannie Shoeman, RN, BS, CLNC, Iowa

I have 15 years of psychiatric nursing in a county hospital, private hospital, group counseling and individual counseling, and I've worked every field of nursing. I had heard about Vickie and, over the years, I'd met nurses who had taken her CLNC® Certification Seminar and become Certified Legal Nurse Consultants^{CM}.

I got my bachelor's degree and went to work for various insurance companies as a workers' comp medical case manager. Then, I worked with managed care insurance until that company went bankrupt and I lost my job.

The insurance company had used nurses in marketing because people would listen to us. We could get our foot in the door, and I realized I was good at it, maybe because of all my years in psych and personal communication.

Working in the Insurance Field Sparked My Interest in the Law

Working in insurance, I became fascinated with the law. When my job ended, I got depressed and gained weight. I decided it was time to try legal nurse consulting, and I went to the *National Alliance of Certified Legal Nurse Consultants (NACLNC®)* Conference to find out more.

However, despite my successful track record in marketing for the insurance company, I discovered how different working for myself was. Making that first call to an attorney was hard. I looked at that long list of attorneys and felt daunted.

I remembered Vickie telling us we'd have to make several calls to get an appointment. I had to remind myself to be confident. At that point in my life confidence did not come easily. I had a lot of personal problems, including a death in the family. My adult son was seriously ill, and supporting him had drained my funds.

Vickie Gave Me the Extra Kick to Start Calling Prospects

I was totally discouraged, but Vickie gave me that extra kick I needed. After the *NACLNC®* Conference, I took the CLNC® Certification Seminar and left the training feeling empowered and full of energy. I now looked at that intimidating list of law firms and decided, "Why shouldn't I go after the really big ones?" I picked out the top ten firms and made the calls.

A woman at the office of a medical malpractice defense attorney said, "Our senior founding partner has thought about hiring a legal nurse consultant. I want you to leave him a personal voice mail."

After a week he called me back. He asked about my resume. My one reference was an attorney who had recently been appointed judge. My prospect said, "I've known Bill for years. Why don't you send me your packet?"

> *The attorney seemed excited introducing me to the other 11 partners. He bragged about my wonderful qualifications and said he planned to hire me as a consultant.*

When I met with the attorney, he seemed excited, taking me around and introducing me to the other 11 partners and the entire staff. He bragged about my wonderful qualifications and said he planned to hire me as a consultant.

My First Case Was a Win for the Attorney and Me

After the meeting nothing happened. I waited three months, thinking he wasn't interested after all. Then he called with the first case. Later, I learned it had taken him that long to get the records.

I had never done medical malpractice or worked for the defense. My experience was with workers' comp and personal injury. This was an involved case, and I was afraid I couldn't do it justice. I told my attorney-client I had an extensive network of CLNC® consultants and could find him a nurse who specialized in that area. However, he wanted me, nobody else. He saw something in me that I didn't. As a result, we both were winners. He won the case, settling for a lot more money because of the information I found in the chart, and I won repeat business.

Since then I've completed six more cases for him. I worked up the last one from inception, billing for 60-plus hours. The checks I received were amazing – $2,500, $5,000, $6,000 – for not that many hours of work.

Vickie gave me that extra kick I needed. I took the CLNC® Certification Seminar and left the training feeling empowered and full of energy.

Vickie's Training Helped Build My Confidence and Discipline

Even though I landed a big firm with those first calls, I still procrastinate doing the marketing. This year, at the *NACLNC®* Conference, a speaker talked about taking one step a day, even if it's small. Vickie's impeccable image also impressed me – it has such punch. I'm still working on building my confidence, and I realize now that looking good and taking that one step every day make me feel more confident.

Using the valuable tips from the *NACLNC®* Conference to build my confidence and discipline, I know I will succeed even more. I believe you have to aim for the top, go for the big one, just like I did when I landed that first top-ten law firm. I love going for it as a Certified Legal Nurse Consultant^CM.

> *I landed a big firm with those first calls. I love going for it as a Certified Legal Nurse Consultant^CM.*

A Life-Altering Twist of Fate Inspired My New Passion as a Certified Legal Nurse Consultant^{CM}

by Jane A. Hurst, RN, CLNC, Ohio

I consider myself Vickie Milazzo Institute's "poster child." My life-altering journey to becoming a successful CLNC® consultant has had its share of ups and downs, and I owe the upswings to Vickie.

I was working as an instructor in an LPN program. I loved my work teaching students about body mechanics. Then I injured myself lifting my dog into the car. I ended up having surgery to repair a herniated disc. A few days postop I began experiencing a new, much more severe pain, yet I couldn't convince the surgeon something wasn't right. He told me I was expecting too much of myself. By the time I was finally admitted to the hospital for additional treatment, complex spinal infections had virtually destroyed two vertebrae, and I also had an epidural abscess.

I knew in my heart I was a victim of malpractice. My career in active clinical nursing was over. I decided to pursue legal action. The attorneys I chose were very good to work with, but they didn't fully understand my clinical picture. They even told me they weren't sure my case would be successful. I felt strongly that because the surgeon wouldn't listen to me, I was paying the price for his poor judgment.

Fortunately, I remembered the Institute's advertisement in a nursing magazine. I decided that if I could learn about the role of a Certified Legal Nurse Consultant^{CM}, I could prove my own case. So in 1992, I sent off for the CLNC® Certification Program. I'll never forget the day that box arrived. I thought I might have bitten off more than I could chew, but I buckled down and studied the whole program. It gave me the confidence to see that I already had all the skills necessary to be a CLNC® consultant – I just needed Vickie to show me the way and redefine that knowledge.

My first case was my own. The lawsuit proceeded successfully, largely because I was able to find research to support my case. I became very involved in the entire process, going to every deposition and being deposed myself. The trial lasted two weeks, and the jury decided in my favor and awarded a large judgment.

I found that I liked what I was doing and set up my home office. Since my physical activity is limited, with my office at home I can lie down when I need to and work when I want to. I consult for the law firm that represented me, and I even got cases from one of the opposing attorneys who deposed me in the suit.

I asked the attorney I'd worked with for so long to write a letter of recommendation for me. Then I

My first case proceeded successfully and the jury awarded a large judgment.

I think of Vickie as the mighty oak tree, and we are all her little seedlings (or maybe little nuts!).

When my fate took a turn, Vickie was there to guide me through. Her words of encouragement and her enthusiasm triggered my drive to purse my new passion.

sent out my promotional packets. The response was great, and I now have new clients.

Back when I was so sick, I wondered what I would do. Nursing was important to me. Thank goodness I am able to use my nursing background in my CLNC® work. I now realize this is exactly what I was meant to do.

We all experience twists of fate in some form. Fortunately, when my fate took a turn, Vickie was there to guide me through. Her words of encouragement and her enthusiasm triggered my drive to pursue my new passion. I think of Vickie as the mighty oak tree, and we are all her little seedlings (or maybe little nuts!).

Trust Your Ability to Rise to the CLNC® Challenge

by Denise Heath-Graham, RN, CLNC, Maryland

In 1995 I became disabled because of a back injury. Vickie's CLNC® Certification Program has been a lifesaver. It allowed me the flexibility to create my own success while being disabled and a new mother.

I started teaching pre-hospital providers how to write legally defensible reports that would keep them out of trouble.

Recently I sold a textbook for the pre-hospital provider, *The Missing Protocol – A Legally Defensible Report*. The first time I promoted my book, it sold out in just over an hour, and people from Alaska to Australia have contacted me about teaching for them.

A huge case against General Motors came from that book. I wanted to tell the attorneys to contact Vickie Milazzo because she is the expert. But Vickie taught me to rise to the challenge so I took the case, and I've been successful ever since.

Legal nurse consulting is now my primary focus. Vickie taught me to pan for gold where there is none. I am very proud to be associated with her. She and Florence Nightingale ought to go down in history together as nursing icons.

Vickie taught me to pan for gold where there is none. I am very proud to be associated with her. She and Florence Nightingale ought to go down in history together as nursing icons.

Exhibiting Kicked Off My CLNC® Business with a Bang!

by Annette Powers-Kilburn, RN, MAOM, CLNC, Ohio

> *The cases are coming in so fast that I hired an office assistant.*

Although I loved working as a registered nurse, becoming the proud owner of two pretty blue titanium rods in my back made 12-hour shifts tough to manage. Being on call 24/7 was no longer possible. I tried it for four months before admitting I had to make a change.

Being a typical class nerd while earning my bachelor's degree, a master's in business and finally becoming an RN, I was used to doing research. In fact, I love research. So when I discovered legal nurse consulting and Vickie Milazzo Institute, I was immediately invested in becoming a Certified Legal Nurse Consultant℠.

The thing that kicked off my CLNC® business was exhibiting at state bar associations. I immediately signed up for four association meetings and was determined to do it right, to have such a professional booth that no one would question whether I'd ever done this before.

Because I'm great at organizing, I checked out all the programs planned for each conference and signed up to participate in every scavenger hunt or door prize drawing. Any opportunity to have attorneys approach me for whatever sticker or stamp they needed would give me the face-to-face interaction I was seeking.

It Worked!

At the Ohio State Bar Association annual meeting, my booth looked professional, and I learned right away to say, "May I trade this sticker for your business card?" Being away from their offices, the attorneys were open to having a conversation. Perfect for me, because having a conversation was exactly what it took to get their attention long enough to explain what I do as a Certified Legal Nurse Consultant^{CM}.

One attorney who came to me at the event said, "I have a friend who's working on a case, and we need an ophthalmology surgeon." "I can take care of that for you," I said, having learned from Vickie that the answer is always yes! "Are you sure you can find one?" he asked. "Absolutely."

The attorney came back to me and brought his friend. Together, they explained the case. "I've already been texting my surgeon," I said, "to see if he'd be interested in looking at your case." That was true – the surgeon happened to be my brother-in-law – but I had reached out to see if he'd be interested and what he would charge. Within four days I located a testifying expert for this attorney-client, and I've received several more cases from him.

Being receptive, positive and responding quickly paid off again at the Kentucky State Bar annual

Being a CLNC® consultant pulls together everything I ever learned as a nurse.

> *What I like best is the independence I have.*

> *To get to my office, I just walk across the driveway.*

meeting. An attorney-prospect approached me to review a case. This morning he sent a text saying he needs my help on three more cases.

A short while after the Kentucky event, I exhibited at the Indiana Solo and Small Firm annual meeting, and I'm scheduled soon for the Michigan meeting. Clearly, exhibiting is growing my CLNC® business. Despite being naturally shy, once I'm face-to-face and doing my job, I get over it. I love talking to people almost as much as I love doing research.

At first the cases trickled in. Now they're coming in so fast that last week I hired an office assistant.

What I Learned from Vickie Milazzo Made This Big Change Possible

I still don't have full sensation in my feet. That takes a long time, a three-year process, and I'm getting there. Fortunately, as a Certified Legal Nurse Consultant^{CM}, I can choose my hours.

Being a CLNC® consultant pulls together everything I ever learned and everything I've experienced as a nurse. It's a unique mix and I love it. Everytime I take on a case I have another opportunity to look at new standards and new information about what's going on in that specialty – a chance to learn more. But what I like best, even more than the research, is the independence I have.

I live on farm land in Covington, Ohio, about an hour from Dayton. My husband installs flooring as an independent contractor, and we lease a big tract of our land to an Amish farmer. When we bought the property, it included a cinder-block structure, which we converted to a house for my in-laws when they were still alive. Now it has become my office.

To get to my office, I just walk across the driveway. Anytime I need a break, I can simply walk outside to enjoy the day. I grab a cup of coffee, a cup of sweet feed and some treats for the chickens, then spend half an hour with our two llamas, getting kisses from Dalai the Llama for a handful of feed. Then I step back into my office, light a candle – unscented, so as not to offend any visitors – change the water on the fresh-cut flowers from the garden and I'm ready to dig into the next case.

I love what I'm doing. At a class reunion recently, a couple of my friends came to me and asked how my business was going. I gave a quick update and they were excited for me. One of them said, "Annette, you've figured out what you want to do with your life. You have that glow." "You mean it shows?" I said. "Oh, my gosh, it shows! You've found your thing. This is what you're supposed to be doing." Yes, I already knew it, but getting that verification felt incredible.

I love what I'm doing.

Getting that verification felt incredible.

Finding the Smoking Gun in a Case Is the Best Feeling Ever

by Caryn "CJ" Jaffe, RN, CLNC, Maryland

As a child, I had Lyme disease. Then in 2004, I was bitten by another tick. Terrible timing, since I'd just gotten married. My symptoms were across the chart, from severe fatigue to periodic paralysis on one side of my body. My husband couldn't handle his wife not walking, not being perfect – so he left and we divorced. A couple of years later, I made it to an Iron Man finish line, so I guess the joke's on him.

Meanwhile, however, my nursing career suffered. An IV therapy nurse walks about seven miles a day, and with Lyme disease I didn't have the energy. In 2007 I still didn't know if I'd ever be able to go back to bedside nursing. As a fallback career that I could do from home, becoming a Certified Legal Nurse Consultant^CM seemed like a good fit. If I could only do nursing part-time, I decided legal nurse consulting might be a good addition.

A friend who was a Certified Legal Nurse Consultant^CM told me Vickie Milazzo Institute was the best. After reading everything I could find, I knew she was right, so I decided to go for it all the way. Every piece of the VIP CLNC® Success System has proved beneficial.

After receiving my CLNC® certification, I immediately got a case. It came through a friend who, of all things, took flying-trapeze lessons with me. With the uncertainty of Lyme disease, I've learned to take my fun when and where I can manage it. Her husband was a medical malpractice and personal injury attorney, so I met with him and told him what I did.

"We have a case that I don't think is meritorious," he said, "but we'd like your professional opinion." He was right, the case had no merit, but I made $500 in 20 minutes. I decided right then that, even though I was sick throughout the CLNC® Certification Seminar, I'd made a great decision investing in Vickie's program.

In 4,000 Pages, I Found the Tiny Smoking Gun

Then, I got really lucky. An in-house Certified Legal Nurse Consultant℠ for a law firm found me through the *NACLNC®* Directory. The woman who called said, "If you would be interested in working as a testifying expert, send me your resume and fee schedule."

Testifying expert? Again, completely out of my comfort zone, but I remembered from class that I could charge more as a testifying expert, and it sounded interesting, so I decided to go for it. I threw $225 an hour out there, and they didn't balk. They overnighted the medical records and a retainer check.

Every piece of the VIP CLNC® Success System has proved beneficial.

After receiving my CLNC® certification, I immediately got a case.

Realizing this was the moment I'd been waiting for, I decided, *I'm giving my all to this case. No matter what happens, whether they select me to testify or not, I'm going to walk away with my head high because I did it right.*

This might sound silly, but I think a nurse should be able to feel important. In my last three or four jobs, I felt I had to cut corners, so I didn't feel I was doing the excellent job I knew I was capable of. As a Certified Legal Nurse Consultant CM, I don't have to cut corners. My job is to be excellent and to find the smoking gun that no one else can see; the one little thing that makes the difference. Feeling this way is the greatest gift ever.

The case I was hired to consult on involves a six-year-old girl who died after her intestines were perforated by a nasoduodenal tube. Improper insertion, we figured, but the documentation was atrocious. The providers documented numerous times that the child had no pain when she died, but I wondered how that was possible. In trying to figure out the pain management (because the way it was laid out in the record made no sense), I created a table of all the child's vital signs.

That's when I found the one thing that would make all the difference in this case. The smoking gun was right there in front of our eyes, but so small it went unnoticed, on a single page of a 4,000-page medical record. I emailed the attorney, "You're not going to believe what I found. The other side might want to settle after this." He was bowled over. "How did you find that? It makes all the difference in this case." Hearing his praise felt so good.

I Owe Everything to Vickie

What a fantastic ride this past couple of months has been. It's proven to me that if I want to be excellent, being a CLNC® consultant is where I can be excellent. There will be competition, but not like at the bedside where I felt ostracized for striving to do a good job. As a Certified Legal Nurse Consultant[CM], I contact another CLNC® consultant and I get help wherever I need it. This is what the whole nursing profession should be. I've landed in the right place, and I'm as happy as I've ever been.

In the Past 6 Weeks, I've Made Twice What I Would Have Made in Bedside Nursing

When I sent the law firm my first bill for this case, $4,500, I wondered if they were going to flip out. But instead I received the check two weeks later. I was so estatic, I framed it.

Then the Certified Legal Nurse Consultant[CM] who had originally contacted me phoned. "The work's just beginning," she said. "My colleague, who is also a CLNC® consultant, and the attorney and I are all impressed with your work product."

What amazes me most is the absolute feeling that this is where I should be, this is what I should have been doing for the past seven years. I'm ready to bill another $10,000 for the work I've done on

I'm ready to bill another $10,000.

this case. It's almost overwhelming to think about, but if my CLNC® business continues like this, I will easily make over $150,000 a year.

Make More Than a Living, Make a Difference

I Set Myself Free by Becoming a Certified Legal Nurse Consultant^{CM}

by Judia Sarich, RN, BSN, CLNC, Texas

Twenty-six months ago I was a burned-out nurse administrator. After working 80+ hours a week for more than five years, I had reached a point of severe sleep deprivation and I was facing potentially serious health issues. I needed to take action. After seeing Vickie Milazzo Institute in every nursing journal, I did.

Becoming a Certified Legal Nurse Consultant^{CM} was not an overnight decision. I prayed for guidance and God sent the answer, but I wanted to make sure. I spent a year checking it out. I laugh about

Vickie's CLNC® Certification Program wasn't costly at all. Most other new businesses far exceed the start-up cost of becoming a CLNC® consultant.

*In writing
the vision
of my
company,
I set
myself free.*

*I take
action on
my business
every day.
The payoffs
have been
great.*

that now because I later learned that Vickie's CLNC® Certification Program wasn't costly at all.

Most other new businesses far exceed the start-up cost of becoming a CLNC® consultant, and other businesses don't include the quality training or the ongoing free support by CLNC® Mentors.

Fourteen months ago I became a Certified Legal Nuse Consultant℠. I love what I do now. More important, I am confident my company's current success is built on a solid foundation and is positioned for dramatic future growth. Why? Because I'm using the building tools Vickie gave me.

I often hear Vickie say, "Write down a detailed vision of your business. Take one action step for your business every day. Use the free support of your CLNC® Mentors. Be creative. Make a commitment to your business." These golden mantras are the cornerstones of my success.

I Carved a Detailed Vision of My CLNC® Future

When I came home from the CLNC® Certification Seminar, I was filled with excitement and determination, but I was at risk of losing all momentum that first week. I had a bad upper respiratory infection. I was so miserable I could have chosen to stay in bed heavily medicated.

Instead, the first thing I did – in between coughing, sneezing and wheezing – was take Vickie's advice: "Write the vision of your company." Vickie's voice was in my head. I wrote, took my antibiotics, used my inhaler, slept, woke up and wrote some more. Despite feeling awful, I built my future CLNC® success, gaining a clear focus on what it would look like. As Antoine de Saint-Exupéry wrote in *The Little Prince*, "A rock pile ceases to be a rock pile the moment a single man contemplates it, bearing within him the image of a cathedral."

This exercise allowed me to see where I was going. Patterning Michelangelo, I saw the angel in the marble and carved until I set him free. The only difference was that, in writing the vision of my company, I set myself free.

Starting Small, I Found Myself Accomplishing Big

Vickie's next cornerstone, "Take one action step for your business every day," became the most important building block of all. This mantra, lodged in my head during the CLNC® Certification Seminar, has carried me through periods when I felt down and worried and through periods when my business was thriving so well I thought I could skip a day. I'm sure Vickie would agree with Zen master Takuan: "This day will not come again. Each minute is worth a priceless gem."

I don't care how big or how small the task is, I take action on my business every day. Some days I talk about my business to someone new, make one new contact call or brainstorm a new marketing strategy. Other days I send a thank-you note or reorganize my office for efficiency.

Not a week goes by that I do not refer to one of the many materials in my VIP CLNC® Success System. Each one has played a part in my company's success.

The power of taking daily action for your business is immense. Many days I didn't feel like doing anything, but I went into the office to do that one thing and by the end of the day I was amazed at how much I had accomplished. The payoffs have been great. All those single action steps are the pebbles that have built my business.

Free CLNC® Mentoring and the *NACLNC®* Association Are My Built-In Support System

Another building block Vickie offers is the Institute's free support – the CLNC Mentors, *NACLNC®* network and the online tools in the *NACLNC®* Association. Not a week goes by that I do not refer to one of the many materials in my VIP CLNC® Success System. I have used each of these great resources, and each one has played a part in my company's success.

The Institute's CLNC® Mentors are supportive, knowledgeable and helpful in every situation. As a new CLNC® consultant making that first client call or setting that first appointment, I found talking to a seasoned CLNC® Mentor invaluable. But these are the obvious times I needed them. Many times the CLNC® Mentors have surpassed my expectations with great responses to unusual questions.

Our *NACLNC® Directory of Certified Legal Nurse Consultants* is another indispensable resource. I have had the opportunity to present several fellow CLNC® peers as testifying expert candidates. I have made a commitment to use only Certified Legal Nurse Consultants^{CM} as nurse testifying experts.

I Now Have the Energy, Time and Ability to Help Others

The final building block is one of the strongest cornerstones of my business. Vickie and more than one of the faculty members at the CLNC® Certification Seminar said, "Be committed to your business." To me this also means be committed to God and give something back to others. I became a nurse because I wanted to make a difference, and I felt I had lost this ability. Now as a CLNC® consultant, I have the energy, time and ability to help others. I am more available to my family, my neighbors, my church and my community. I have time to participate in a volunteer organization that helps a local home for the mentally challenged.

How different my life is today. I'm busy and my days are full, but balanced, not chaotic. I am in charge of my life and my business. My work environment is healthy. There's no traffic to fight, no unproductive meetings to attend. I love my home office work space and using technology to reach out to clients across the nation. I have attorney-clients in California, Utah, Wyoming and Texas.

I have found balance and fulfillment in my life again. Thanks to Vickie Milazzo, the visionary pioneer whose fearless leadership and willingness to share have made such an impact on me and thousands of other nurses, I am a successful Certified Legal Nurse Consultant℠. I'm proud to be a CLNC® consultant. As Vickie says, "We Are Nurses and We Can Do Anything!®"

> *How different my life is. I'm busy, but balanced, not chaotic. I am in charge of my life and my business.*

> *I have attorney-clients in California, Utah, Wyoming and Texas.*

Just 2 Months After I Became a Certified Legal Nurse Consultant[CM] I Landed My First Big Client

by Melanie V. Paquette,
RN, BSN, CLNC, Texas

For the first two months, nothing was happening. What was I doing wrong? My husband said, "Give it a chance, Melanie. Let me help."

He began calling the attorneys I had sent postcards to, and he got results. He booked me for presentations at law firms where I discovered that face-to-face interaction is my strong suit. Once an attorney agrees to a presentation, and I show what I can do, closing the sale is a given.

My first big client, however, came by way of a referral from my insurance agent. My agent's neighbor is an attorney who referred his medical malpractice and personal injury cases to another attorney. That's when I found out how useful it is to know people who know people who know people. He passed my name along, and I got a call.

"What can you do for us?" the attorney asked.

Boy, did I answer that question. Amazingly, their firm hadn't used legal nurse consultants. Their paralegal was pulling her hair out, unable to provide what they needed.

In closing I asked, "When may I come to your office and show you what I can do?"

> *Our business has grown so fast. We make $5,000-$6,000 per month and have already replaced my husband's salary.*

> *This single attorney-client can keep me busy full time.*

The Work Started Flowing and We Replaced My Husband's Salary

I handle all of that attorney-client's cases, including medical malpractice, personal injury and workers' comp. This single attorney-client can keep me busy full time, but my goal is to grow big enough to hire CLNC® subcontractors. We're almost there. We have four attorney-clients now – and the work keeps flowing.

I say "we" now because my husband left his job and came to work for me full time as an office manager. That was one of the smartest moves I made. A disabled veteran, he's able to take care of our children and still help with our marketing. He also answers the phone, which means an attorney gets a live voice, not an answering machine.

Being responsive is one important reason our business has grown so fast. We make $5,000-$6,000 per month and have already replaced my husband's salary.

I Like Educating Attorneys – Once They Know You, They Need You

The most amazing thing happens when I give a presentation at a law firm: attorneys pay attention. I wow them with the CLNC® services I can provide to help them win cases and they treat me as a professional. I use their feedback to refine my presentation for the next time I deliver it.

After attorneys learn what a CLNC® consultant can do for them, they see the value. Later, when I actually work with them, they begin to rely on me

> "I wow them with the CLNC® services I can provide to help them win cases and they treat me as a professional."

in more and more areas, on more and more cases. Just recently, our biggest attorney-client emailed us to say we had become their best friends and they cannot function without us.

One thing I learned from Vickie is to hold my ground on nonmeritorious cases. That principle is working for me. After I review a case, my client will ask, "Melanie, what's your recommendation? What do I do with this?"

If the case has merit, fine. I lay it out. But I sometimes have to say, "I understand that something bad happened, and your client is upset about it, but I don't see merit here." In the long run, the attorney saves money by not pursuing cases he can't win.

My attorney-clients listen to me and respect my judgment. That makes me feel that my nursing experience and knowledge are making a difference.

While taking my CLNC® training, I came up with the slogan we use in our marketing: *We make you look best.* My attorney-clients love it.

I Enjoy What I Do Every Day

Being a nurse is important to me, and my CLNC® business makes me happy in many ways I never expected. I enjoy my attorney-client relationships. I enjoy feeling that I'm still helping people, even though it isn't at the bedside.

On every case, I learn something new, which I can then use on future cases. That's exciting. While I'm teaching my attorney-clients about medical records and the healthcare side of a situation, they're handling the legal side and I'm learning from them, too. Together, we make a brilliant team. I help identify issues that will help them look good in the courtroom and win the cases that deserve to be won.

I also enjoy knowing that my children are not spending time at daycare. I used to feel guilty about leaving them, but now they're getting the best care at home with their father. My CLNC® business has positively impacted our entire family.

After serving his country in Iraq, my husband came home with limitations that make it hard for him to work outside the home. I created a job for him, and he's a valuable asset to my CLNC® business. No one could do a better job running the office, and I love working with him. This could never have happened if I'd stayed full time at the hospital. I'm proud that ours is a family business, that we can grow it together.

Recently, I've begun traveling for my attorney-clients, which is another exciting aspect of what I do. On one case, the attorney requested that I meet with his client who needed to be assessed for a life care plan. When I asked the attorney if he wanted me to find someone local to assess his client in order to save on travel cost, he insisted that I go myself because of the quality of my work. I was flattered. My office-manager husband made all the travel arrangements for me to fly in early one morning and come back the same day. This was a wonderful experience! I had never had a frequent flyer card before now. I feel professional!

Being a nurse is important to me, and my CLNC® business makes me happy in many ways I never expected.

Vickie's a tiny lady but powerful. She looks at you like you're the only person on the planet.

We Keep Marketing Smart to Attract New Attorney-Clients Like Vickie Taught Us

One day we drove past a billboard for a law firm that specializes in personal injury cases. I told my husband, "We should call on them." He called and booked me for a presentation.

That's the sort of marketing that gets big results at low cost. This month we'll be mailing out and following up on a hundred postcards.

We offer a discount on the first case. Attorneys are like anybody else when it comes to saving money. The discount encourages them to take a chance, and it costs us nothing until a prospect actually hires us. We do a great job, the client is impressed and hires us again at our full rate. Marketing can be effective without draining your bank account – Vickie taught me that too.

Vickie Made It All Possible

I feel very lucky to have been trained by Vickie Milazzo. She's amazing. When I completed the CLNC® Certification Program, I told my husband, "Vickie's a tiny lady but powerful. She looks at you like you're the only person on the planet. The world around her stops and she listens to you, giving you her time and all her attention."

It has been a year now since my CLNC® Certification. A very happy year. I think back to those first two months, when I doubted myself, and I have to laugh. My life has changed in so many wonderful ways since I became a Certified Legal Nurse ConsultantCM.

Success *and* Time with My Children Are Possible as a Certified Legal Nurse Consultant^{CM}

by Arnita Christie, RN, BSN, MS, CLNC, Connecticut

I transitioned from bedside clinical nursing into sales with the last eight years in pharmaceutical sales. But I always wanted to be independent and own my own business, while being able to spend more time with my children. I'd seen Vickie Milazzo Institute's advertisements in the nursing journals for many years, and I believed the CLNC® Certification Program would give me the chance to achieve my goal of owning my own business. I wanted to learn from the pioneer so I would be totally comfortable with the attorneys' language and my responsibilities as a CLNC® consultant.

I enrolled in the CLNC® Certification Seminar and the *NACLNC*® 2-Day Apprenticeship. In the seminar, I received a great deal of information, and the 2-Day Apprenticeship put it all together and showed me how to market, interview with attorneys and write actual case reports. Receiving hands-on experience helped tremendously in activating my 90-day marketing plan. Within two months, I had my first case, a workers' compensation case.

With the CLNC® Marketing Templates I Was Ready to Get Started on Day One

What helped me succeed was really listening when Vickie talked about developing a plan, writing

> *The 2-Day Apprenticeship put it all together and showed me how to market, interview with attorneys and write actual case reports. Within two months, I had my first case.*

down goals and taking an action step every day. I also prayed a lot.

When I returned home from the CLNC® Certification Seminar, I looked at my 90-day marketing plan and said, "I need to do something every day." First, I sent out more than 150 emails to everyone I knew. I explained that I was a Certified Legal Nurse Consultant℠ and asked for attorney referrals. I received numerous responses, and I began working on those referrals.

My CLNC® Marketing Template materials were right there for me so I was able to begin marketing immediately. Not having to create and design my promotional package saved me many hours and thousands of dollars.

Next, I went online and researched the various attorney referrals I'd received. Then I did what Vickie taught me: I practiced in front of a mirror, I practiced in front of my kids and in front of my husband. I picked up that phone and I called the attorneys to request an interview. I ended up with a couple of phone conversations and four attorney appointments.

Vickie and the CLNC® Mentors Guide Me Every Step of the Way

With my CLNC® training and my nursing experience, I'm able to review and analyze a medical chart, and provide my attorney-clients not only with information about what's in the chart, but also with information about what's missing that they might not notice.

I absolutely recommend the CLNC® Certification Program to anyone even thinking about reviewing medical cases or working with attorneys. Vickie is magnetic and her words just grab you. She speaks from the heart – nurse-to-nurse. This program is designed specifically for us. You have to be a nurse to appreciate that. Vickie's education and the CLNC® Mentoring Program made launching my CLNC® business achievable for me.

Attorneys speak a different language than nurses. So I wanted a support system, and the Institute's program provides me with that. I use the CLNC® Mentors in all parts of my business, from my television interview to my first case, to any new hurdles. The CLNC® Mentors gave me suggestions about what to review before the TV interview and they have coached me on every aspect of my cases. I haven't taken a step without them. Having an energetic mentor like Vickie and the unlimited CLNC® Mentoring I receive as a VIP are priceless.

My next step will be offering my services as a speaker to the state bar association. I plan to inform the attorneys about new trends affecting their cases from the medical perspective and the resulting pitfalls their clients may face. This will give me a platform for describing my CLNC® services and showing how I can assist on their legal teams in dealing with these issues.

They have coached me on every aspect of my cases. Having an energetic mentor like Vickie and the unlimited CLNC® Mentoring I receive as a VIP are priceless.

I Can Advocate for Patients and My Children at a New Level

Today, I'm a full-time Certified Legal Nurse Consultant^{CM}*, and I'm able to participate in my children's lives. Just as important as being there for my family, I can also help pay the mortgage.*

One of the best things about my CLNC® business is helping. Even as a little girl, I wanted to help people. My mom said that if I saw a tattered doll, I'd try to fix it or put a Band-Aid® on it. That helping spirit is inside me. Now, I help people in a different way. As a bedside nurse, you're a patient advocate. As a CLNC® consultant, I'm able to support my attorney-clients while upholding the standards of care for nursing.

The best personal benefit of becoming a CLNC® consultant has been finding balance in my life. I'm the proud mother of two small children, and it is important to me to be active in their education and after-school programs. Working 50 to 60 hours a week, whether in nursing or in pharmaceutical sales, did not allow me to do that.

When you have children, balance is essential – not just working all the time – because you cannot get back the years of their youth. Today, I'm a full-time Certified Legal Nurse Consultant^{CM}, and I'm able to participate in my children's lives. That's what having my own CLNC® business has provided me. Just as important as being there for my family, I can also help pay the mortgage.

Thank you, Vickie, for everything.

You'll Know It When You Find It – And I Found It as a Certified Legal Nurse Consultant℠!

by Suzi Sharp, RN, BSN, CLNC, Washington

I've been in nursing for 37 years, so I've done a zillion things – medical-surgical, pediatrics, OB/GYN, geriatrics, orthopedics, family practice, home health, hospice care, intravenous therapy and emergency care. I've lived and worked on an Indian reservation and even spent a month in Afghanistan. I took early retirement, but after about a year I was ready to *do* something. Retirement stinks! I considered nursing jobs, but I didn't want to do that anymore. Plus, I didn't want to work for peanuts, and the stock market slump had eaten a large portion of my retirement nest egg. I wanted to do something I loved that would pay me what I'm worth.

One day, I told my eldest son, the "artist," that I didn't know what to do with myself. He said, "Mom, don't worry about it. Just lay back. It'll come to you and you'll know it when it comes."

Vickie's CLNC® Certification Program Cured My "Retirement Blues"

About that time I saw a colorful ad in a nursing publication. That's when I learned about Vickie Milazzo Institute's CLNC® Certification Program.

I didn't know much about legal nurse consulting, although I had been deposed and testified as a

> *On one huge case I earned more than $10,000. I made a total of $25,000 in the next three months, and I was in business from then on.*

witness a few times. My main connection with the law was my father. I grew up in a courtroom because my dad was an attorney, and he often took me with him. There wasn't anything better than going to court and watching him in action.

Vickie's ad about becoming a Certified Legal Nurse Consultant[CM] fascinated me. I requested information and I checked out the Institute's website, all the while thinking, "This sounds too good to be true. What's the catch?" I talked to my other son, the "practical" stock broker, who said, "What do you have to lose?"

I still had some money stashed away so I went to the CLNC® Certification Seminar. I loved the great professional training and I was so glad I did it. I was really excited when I learned I had become certified, because the CLNC® Exam was tough. In fact, I'm looking forward to attending the next *National Alliance of Certified Legal Nurse Consultants* (*NACLNC®*) Conference, because with Vickie there, I know I'll get pumped up, and there's no certification exam at the end.

A month after attending the CLNC® Certification Seminar, I produced a business plan, had a logo designed and business cards printed. I developed an attractive website and started advertising in a local attorney newspaper. I began marketing by calling attorneys, sending out information packets and following up on leads.

About that time, I was invited to go to Afghanistan for a month to help with medical services. I was thrilled and began preparing to leave the country.

Three Cases Started My Success Snowball Rolling

A week before my departure, two attorneys called and wanted to hire me for their cases. Two days later a third attorney called. Fortunately, all of them (three attorneys in three different cities) agreed to wait for me to return from Afghanistan.

When I got back home, I started my CLNC® career in earnest with these three cases. One was a huge case for which I eventually reviewed more than a thousand pages of records and earned more than $10,000. I made a total of $25,000 in the next three months, and I was in business from then on.

Other attorneys are now discovering that I offer a valuable professional service. They know I'm thorough, reliable and trustworthy and I take my work seriously. The CLNC® Certification Program has really paid off. My legal nurse consulting practice continues to grow.

My Nursing Know-How Makes a Big Difference in My CLNC® Cases

As a Certified Legal Nurse Consultant^{CM}, you can generate work for yourself once you learn the medical circumstances of a case. For example, one of my attorney-clients represented a young Native American woman who lived on a reservation and whose medical situation was being judged unfairly. I looked more closely into her records

I'm looking forward to attending the next NACLNC® Conference, because with Vickie there, I know I'll get pumped up.

The CLNC® Certification Program has really paid off.

*A CLNC®
consultant
can make
a big
difference
in a case.
By citing
medical
aspects the
attorneys
hadn't
noticed,
I have
just about
handed
them
what they
needed to
win several
cases.*

and pointed out some medical issues the attorney hadn't considered. He told me to find an expert witness to testify to the special circumstances of the case. By following my nursing instincts and asking pertinent questions, I shed a whole new light on the case and generated more business for myself. Most important, I pointed out extenuating medical conditions that warranted a larger financial settlement for the young woman.

A CLNC® consultant can make a big difference in a case. By citing medical aspects the attorneys hadn't noticed, I have just about handed them what they needed to win several cases.

For example, I worked for the defense on a major case involving a man's alleged sexual abuse of his daughter. The now-adult woman supposedly had childhood memories of the abuse. After poring over the records for 2½ months, seven days a week and most evenings, and reviewing about 1,000 pages of charts, I discovered she was a prescription drug addict and had told different stories about the alleged assaults to different counselors. In addition to my comprehensive report, I wrote a three-page summary of my findings. When my attorney-client read the summary, he asked, "Can you back up everything you've reported?" I said, "Of course." He exclaimed, "Holy cow! We've just won this case!" As a CLNC® consultant, sometimes you do more than provide direction on the case with your nursing experience – sometimes you have major impact on the outcome.

I feel so good about what I do. I just love it. The cases are so much fun, so interesting and so challenging, I don't notice the clock. I can work at my own pace and there's no mandatory overtime.

Vickie's CLNC® Training Put Me on an Equal Footing with Attorneys

When I was getting ready to retire, I thought, "What a waste not to use the nursing knowledge and experience I've gained during the past 35 years." Now, I not only get to use my knowledge, but I can also increase it. When people ask what a Certified Legal Nurse Consultant^{CM} does, I usually tell them, "Certified Legal Nurse Consultants^{CM} get to sleuth through medical charts. It's like being a detective."

Vickie gives us the training and insight to deal with attorneys on an equal footing. She tells us repeatedly, "You will know how to do the job." And she's right. At first I felt lost, but then I remembered what Vickie says: Attorneys may be the masters of the law, but as a CLNC® consultant, I'm the master of the medical chart. As I followed her lead, I not only got the job done, but I also built a lot of self-confidence. I now know how necessary we as Certified Legal Nurse Consultants^{CM} are and how good we can be for a case.

Soon I'm meeting with a firm that has 40 personal injury attorneys. I'm going to walk in that door thinking, "Just give me a case and I'll show you what I can do."

> *I feel so good about what I do. I just love it. The cases are so much fun, so interesting and so challenging, I don't notice the clock. I can work at my own pace and there's no mandatory overtime.*

I have tremendous admiration, respect and gratitude for Vickie. She is so genuine and passionate about helping nurses become CLNC® successes, and her enthusiasm motivates and inspires others. I also like the Institute's CLNC® Mentoring Program. The CLNC® Mentors always increase my knowledge. I just wish I had discovered Vickie's program sooner.

My son told me I'd know what to do with myself when I found it, and he was right. I've found myself as a CLNC® consultant, and I can do this until I'm 92!

One Phone Call Mushroomed Into My Full-Time CLNC® Business

by Susan Porter, RNC, BS, CLNC, South Carolina

I have 33 years of nursing experience in several different fields. A few years ago my husband saw an advertisement for Vickie Milazzo Institute in one of the nursing magazines and said I'd be good at legal nurse consulting.

We had recently adopted a special needs infant and it was three years before I could feel comfortable being away from home. Then I enrolled in the CLNC® Certification Program and became a Certified Legal Nurse Consultant℠.

My husband, who's always my motivating factor, started sending out promotional materials to attorneys. He said, "You need to start answering your phone with Susan Porter and Associates."

Thanks to Vickie I Knew Exactly What to Say When the First Attorney Called

One week after my letters and brochures went out, I was taking my daughter to school when my phone rang. I answered "Susan Porter and Associates." The voice on the other end said, "This is Mary Sue. I'm an attorney. I received your CLNC® information packet and I have a home health case that I think you'd be perfect for."

"Thanks to the CLNC® Certification Program, I knew exactly what to say so when the attorney asked what my fees were – I said '$150 an hour.' She said, 'That's perfect.'"

After my first case, I cut back to one day every two weeks at the hospital. In just months my CLNC® business mushroomed.

It only took my first two cases to pay for the VIP CLNC® Success System.

I had to pull over to the side of the road and take a deep breath – she was actually interviewing me on the phone. Thanks to the CLNC® Certification Program, I knew exactly what to say so when the attorney asked what my fees were – I said, "$150 an hour." She said, "That's perfect." We set up a meeting the following week, and in the meantime, she sent me the records to review.

When I went to her office, I learned that this was the largest defense firm in my hometown in South Carolina. The firm has five partners and 14 attorneys. I left with two more cases from their office, and another attorney from the firm soon called me on a new case.

After my first case, I cut back to one day every two weeks at the hospital. In just months my CLNC® business mushroomed. A defense attorney who switched to plaintiff work asked me to continue reviewing his cases.

In one of the cases, the hospital involved was sold. A different law firm took over their case and asked me to send my final bill. I thought the case was dead for me, but the attorney who picked it up called from North Carolina and asked if he could meet with me. We met, and he asked me to continue reviewing the case, which settled two days before going to court. He also referred me to a colleague in North Carolina.

I just got another referral from an attorney in the original law firm whom I hadn't even met.

I Paid for My VIP CLNC® Success System in Two Cases

My CLNC® business was mushrooming and I was exhilarated. It only took my first two cases to pay for the VIP CLNC® Success System.

I don't know how anybody could be a legal nurse consultant without taking the CLNC® Certification Program. Without it I would not have known what to do or where to begin. I still review the *Core Curriculum for Legal Nurse Consulting*® textbook with every case.

The CLNC® Mentors are invaluable. I had so many things to ask and I wanted to make sure I was on the right track. The CLNC Mentors are always there to help, and every question is handled professionally.

I also attended the *NACLNC*® 2-Day Apprenticeship, where I learned to apply the principles in the CLNC® Certification Program and the *Core Curriculum*. The Apprenticeship gave me the skills to think on my feet with attorneys. Role playing was especially helpful. I was able to see a case in action and experience what it would be like before I went home and tried it myself.

Staying Visible to the Attorneys Keeps Me Successful

From the time I received that first phone call, I made a point of being visible to the attorneys, like Vickie taught us. Even when they gave me the job over the phone I still went in, introduced

> *I don't know how anybody could be a legal nurse consultant without taking the CLNC® Certification Program. Without it I would not have known what to do or where to begin.*

myself and made face-to-face contact. I've met all the attorneys I've worked with and know their assistants by name. When I offered to send my CV to the attorney on my latest case, he said, "That's okay. If you're good enough for Mary Sue, that's all I need." But I'll still go by and introduce myself so he'll know who he's working with.

Consistent marketing means better visibility. Because I market myself consistently, I know exactly what's in the presentation packet I send to each attorney. Even when I talk to an attorney on the phone, I can visualize what's in front of him and I can discuss my CLNC® services effectively.

I also stay visible by following up after I start my review. I call to let the attorney know what I've accomplished. That way, if there's some time between contacts, she knows I'm still out there working on the case.

The CLNC® Certification Program taught me that staying visible often presents unexpected marketing opportunities. So, as Vickie teaches us, I took some time out of my schedule to go to the courthouse to watch a malpractice case one of my defense attorney-clients was trying. During the lunch break the plaintiff attorney approached me and asked why I was there. I explained what I did, and he said, "I could have used your services on this case," which he eventually lost. I gave him my card and offered to help on his next case. Every situation is an opportunity to market and courthouses are where the attorneys are.

As a CLNC® Consultant I Set My Own Hours and Work at My Own Pace

My favorite part of being a Certified Legal Nurse Consultant℠ is reviewing the chart and determining if the standards of care have been adhered to. The Institute's training and my years of experience as a nurse give me the confidence to know I'm doing the job right. Working as a Certified Legal Nurse Consultant℠ is fascinating and exciting. I also feel like I'm making a difference by determining whether the case has merit and by educating the attorney about the medical issues of the case so he can present it to the jury in a way they can understand.

I like the independence of setting my own hours and working at my own pace. Often I'm working after my children go to sleep at night and after I take them to school during the day. This flexibility allows me to accomplish everything I need to do.

Vickie's teaching style is very entertaining and motivating, yet easy to understand. Vickie presents the CLNC® Certification Seminar in a way that you never lose interest. When you have completed the program, you're ready to get started. She makes you believe you can do it because you're a nurse. And she's right when she says, "We are nurses and we can do anything!®"

Vickie presents the CLNC® Certification Seminar in a way that you never lose interest.

When you have completed the program, you're ready to get started.

How I Earn Six Figures as a Certified Legal Nurse Consultant^{CM}

by Kris Wilder, RN, BSN, CLNC, Pennsylvania

I followed Vickie's process. Less than two years after becoming a CLNC® consultant, my income with bonus is more than six figures.

I absolutely love what I do. Every day, I wake up excited to go to work.

I had no idea the industry of legal nurse consulting existed, yet I was interested in the legal world even before I became a nurse. One day eight years into my career, I was talking to a coworker. "I love nursing," I told her, "but the legal aspects of what we do intrigues me too. I wish I could find a way to do both."

She immediately pulled up Vickie Milazzo Institute's website, LegalNurse.com. "Why don't you do this?" I read it, slept on it and a week later I was sitting in the CLNC® Certification Seminar with Vickie and obtaining my CLNC® Certification.

I met a nice mix of RNs there. A few were renewing their CLNC® Certification but hadn't yet done much. I had to wonder if they were taking their legal nurse consulting business seriously. Why go to the trouble of training and getting certified if you aren't going to put everything into it? I also met a number of Certified Legal Nurse Consultants^{CM} who were quite successful. What I learned from this eclectic group was success is not going to fall in your lap: "You have to work for it. If you do what Vickie teaches, it definitely comes together."

Two Career Choices (Nursing and Legal) Melded in a Way I Never Dreamed Possible

As a nurse, I understand medical records. It's easy to tell what's legit, what's not, what is the standard of care and what's not so common. As a Certified Legal Nurse Consultant℠, it's extremely interesting to see the legal view and how the two fields merge and interact.

After being certified my big challenge was finding my place. I wanted to work as an in-house CLNC® consultant. I saw an ad for a corporate nurse consultant that sounded interesting, so I applied. The company interviewed nurses for three full days, some with far more experience than I had. My specialties were emergency, urgent care and case management, which included a supervisory position. I had my master's degree, but so did many other RNs. On the negative side, I had no experience in workers' compensation, which was a key qualification. On the positive side, I was a Certified Legal Nurse Consultant℠.

"The deciding factor," my new director told me later, "was your certification as a legal nurse consultant. Not one of the other applicants had it."

The entire experience has been phenomenal. I have autonomy, which I love, and flexible work hours. I can work from home if I wish.

Every Day Brings a New Case and a Fascinating New Experience

Being the manager for workers' compensation might not sound sexy, but it's my dream job. And I could not have landed it without my CLNC® Certification. The corporation manufactures and

'The deciding factor,' my new director told me later, 'was your certification as a legal nurse consultant. Not one of the other applicants had it.'

supplies paints, coatings, optical products, specialty materials, glass and fiber glass. It has seven divisions with plants, distribution centers and retail stores around the world.

I'm in charge of the architectural coatings division and responsible for about 8,000 employees in the U.S. and Puerto Rico. I manage all of the workers' comp and short-term disability claims as well as the return-to-work process.

Today I had a motor vehicle accident to review and also a knee injury case from a slip and fall. All of the workplace injuries occurring in my division come to my desk, from minor lacerations, shoulder strains and knee injuries to catastrophic traumas. I work to make sure each claim is a valid workers' comp claim. I interact closely with the adjuster and our third-party administrator to gather information and records. Then I review past history and prior medical records for any pre-existing conditions that have contributed to this injury. I also work with physicians to expedite the return to work, or where indicated, to lift some of the restrictions that they have placed on the employee.

One challenging case involves an alleged back injury resulting from assembling a display. The instructions clearly stated that assembling the display is a two-person job, yet the worker did the assembly by himself. He didn't follow protocol or procedure and wasn't even wearing appropriate shoes. The incident report was not filed in a timely manner, nor did the employee follow my direction to seek care. The employee says his claim is work related, but my assessment is that it probably isn't. The employee's actions appear a bit suspicious, and he has become nonresponsive to human resources. Now I'm working with our attorneys because the worker will probably seek legal counsel.

Investigating the Workers' Compensation Cases Is the Best Part of My Legal Nurse Consulting Job

Going through his chart, I made sure our chronological times were accurate. It's been fascinating working this case from beginning to end. From my point of view, it's a lot of investigating, and investigation is fun.

Career has always been a major focus for my life. When I was an RN, whatever my position at the time, I was always searching for what else was out there. I wanted something more. Now, as a Certified Legal Nurse Consultant^{CM}, I use my skills in an atypical way. I don't work for attorneys, although I interact with them.

This job already feels like it's exactly the right fit. I'm completely at ease interacting with attorneys on the issues of a case. I save my company money and protect them from wrongful claims, but I also support our employees, making sure they get the proper care and consideration, both medical and legal. It's a rewarding and unique way to use both my nursing and legal training. I consider this my "final resting place." I'll be here for life.

The entire experience has been phenomenal. I have autonomy, which I love, and flexible work

Being the manager for workers' compensation is my dream job. And I could not have landed it without my CLNC® Certification.

hours that start any time between 7:00am and 9:00am and finish accordingly. Also, I can work from home if I wish. The best part, though, is the investigation.

I love digging into a chart to determine whether the claim is legitimate or not and I assess how best to manage the medical care. Am I defending an employee with a valid claim or protecting the company from a fraudulent one?

I Wouldn't Have This Phenomenal Opportunity Without Vickie Milazzo Institute's CLNC® Training

It's pretty neat how it all has worked out. Most Certified Legal Nurse Consultants^CM go the entrepreneurial route, which I didn't want to do. In every other way, however, I followed Vickie's process.

On the cover of my notebook, which I used in the CLNC® Certification Seminar, I wrote one of Vickie's quotes. She said, "Do something for your CLNC® business every day." Literally, I did that, whether it was looking online for a job, making an outreach call, touching base or selecting a new business outfit, I did something every day.

Less than two years after becoming certified as a CLNC® consultant, my income with bonus is six figures. And I absolutely love what I do. Every day, I wake up excited to go to work.

I'm completely at ease interacting with attorneys on the issues of a case.

The Role of the Certified Legal Nurse Consultant^{CM}

From the Official CLNC® Certification Textbook: *Core Curriculum for Legal Nurse Consulting®*

by Vickie L. Milazzo, RN, MSN, JD

W e encourage you to watch the complete Module 1: The Role of the Certified Legal Nurse Consultant^{CM} video. To enroll in this free 3½-hour online video course visit LegalNurse.com/free-video. You'll experience The Role of the Certified Legal Nurse Consultant^{CM} from the CLNC® Certification Program first hand. Complete the free program and receive 4 contact hours FREE.

> *This excellent intro has given me great insights on what to expect with the CLNC® Certification Program. I like Vickie's teaching style. She is so straight to the point.*
> — Natasha Wilson, RN

Vickie Milazzo Legal Nurse Consulting

7 Types of Cases on Which Certified Legal Nurse Consultants^{CM} Are Qualified to Consult

Medical and Nursing Malpractice Cases

These cases involve the professional negligence of a healthcare provider or the negligence of a healthcare facility or learning institution.

They also involve the negligence of an individual or entity who makes decisions regarding access to care.

- Delay of treatment.
- Inappropriate use of utilization review.
- Negligent case management.

General Personal Injury Cases

Nonprofessional negligence cases are commonly referred to as personal injury or PI cases.

Technically, PI includes malpractice, although attorneys usually distinguish between medical malpractice and other negligence not involving healthcare professionals.

Examples of personal injury cases include:

- Auto accident cases.
- Premises liability cases (e.g., slip and fall, high-stacking injuries, sexual assault, physical assault cases).
- Theme park cases.
- Aviation cases.
- Liquor liability cases.
- Railroad cases.
- Admiralty and maritime cases.
- Water accident cases.
- Sports injury cases.
- Toxic mold cases.
- Dog bite cases.

Products Liability Cases

These cases include claims brought for personal injury, death or property damage caused by the manufacture, construction, design, formulation, preparation, assembly, installation, testing, warnings, instructions, marketing, packaging or labeling of any product.

Medical device and drug-related products liability cases include:

- Celebrex®.
- Bextra®.
- Avandia®.

Amazing module. Vickie is an excellent speaker who makes the information easy to understand. Now I am sure I want to pursue legal nurse consulting.

– Lynn Motz, RN

- Hormone therapy.
- Birth control pills
- Vioxx®.
- Ephedrine.
- Oxycontin®.
- Accutane.
- Botox®.
- Fosamax®.
- Dilantin®.
- Hip implants (all metal).
- Implantable defibrillators.
- Pacemakers.
- Industrial-grade silicone breast implants.
- Ventilators.
- Heart valves.
- IV pumps.

Nonmedical device products liability cases include:

- Machinery and equipment.
- Children's toys and products.
- Cigarettes and cigarette lighters.
- Motor vehicles, automobiles and automobile parts.
- Food.
- Household products.
- Personal care products.
- Consumer products (e.g., appliances).
- Industrial products.

Toxic Tort and Environmental Cases

These cases involve alleged damages or injuries caused by the release of toxins into the environment.

Examples of toxic tort and environmental cases include cases involving toxins from:

- Oil spills.
- Waste products from manufacturing processes.
- Electromagnetic fields (e.g., against a utility company).
- Radiation contamination.
- Hazardous chemicals in a workplace.
- Waste management and disposal.
- Pesticides.
- Sick building syndrome.
- Lead poisoning.

Workers' Compensation and Workplace Injury Cases

These cases involve job-related injuries, i.e., injuries that arise out of and in the course of employment. A claimant must show that he suffered an impairment or incapacity that rendered him unable to earn the wages he was being paid when he sustained the injury in the same or other employment.

Examples of workers' comp cases include:

- Equipment- and machinery-related injuries.
- Cumulative trauma disorders.
- Injuries caused by objects striking workers.
- Back injuries.
- Auto accidents.

I feel enthusiastic again about my future nursing career. Vickie makes it seem doable and fun. I feel like I've found my niche.

– JoAnn Hennessy, RN

Criminal Cases

A crime is any act that society has deemed contrary to the public good. The act must be injurious to society to be considered a crime.

Differences between civil and criminal cases are as follows:

- Personal versus social.
  - Civil actions are personal in nature, cause individual harm, personal injury or property damage, and result in monetary damages.
  - Criminal actions are deemed against all of society, violating the peace and tranquility of the community.
- Type of act.
  - Civil cases involve a cause of action from which the injury arises.
  - Criminal cases involve homicide, assault, rape or abuse, among others.
- Proof required.
  - Civil cases require proof by a preponderance of the evidence.
  - Criminal cases require proof beyond a reasonable doubt.
- Verdict required.
  - A civil verdict requires a majority of the jury (usually 10 of 12) to agree.
  - A criminal verdict must be unanimous.
- Some actions can be both criminal and civil.

Certified Legal Nurse Consultants[CM] can consult on these various criminal cases and more:

- Driving while intoxicated (DWI)/driving under the influence (DUI) cases.
- Sexual and physical assault cases.
- Child, spouse or elderly abuse cases.
- Criminal cases against individual providers and facilities.
- Criminal environmental cases.
- Any case involving a victim of a violent crime.
- Psychiatric defenses and psychiatric issues.
- Medicaid and medicare fraud and abuse cases.
- Possession of narcotics cases.
- Excessive use of force by law enforcement cases.

Any Case Where Health, Illness or Injury Is an Issue

Certified Legal Nurse Consultants^CM are qualified to answer questions, research topics and assist attorneys in developing the medical-related issues of many types of cases.

Examples of such cases include:

- Family law (e.g., custody battle).
- Probate (e.g., competency in issue).
- School health (e.g., injury of a child while crossing the street, sexual assault by a teacher).
- Americans with Disabilities Act (ADA).
- Employer-employee relationships (e.g., wrongful dismissal).
- Sexual harassment.

This free module is very impressive, professionally done and packed with great information. It provided just what I was looking for as I explore becoming a Certified Legal Nurse Consultant^CM.

– Jonell Alme, RN, BSN, PHN

- Right to die.
- Social Security benefit issues.
- Medicare benefit issues.
- Physician-facility relationships (e.g., physician dropped from an HMO, preferred provider network or managed care network).
- Psychiatrist or therapist abuse or injury.
- Insurance issues (e.g., reasonableness of a medical bill, relationship of a medical bill to the alleged damages or injuries).
- Family Leave Act.
- Bad faith litigation against insurance companies for failure to pay a claim or for denial of access to specific care or treatment.
- Wrongful adoption.
- Healthcare professional board disciplinary actions.

Very interesting! I think I've found my new career path!

– Laura Hoffman, RN, BSN

Distinctions Between the Testifying Expert (TE) and the Consulting Expert (CE)

Summary of Distinctions

Testifying Expert	Consulting Expert
An expert who is expected to testify at deposition or trial.	An expert who is *not* expected to testify, but consults with attorney-client behind the scenes, preps attorney and helps attorney develop the case.

Testifying Expert	Consulting Expert
Testimony is limited to areas of professional expertise.	Can review and analyze *all aspects* of a variety of cases. No limitations on the scope of consultation.
Work product is generally discoverable.	Work product is generally *not* discoverable.

Implications of Distinctions

Expectations.

- Both types of consultants can provide similar services, but a Certified Legal Nurse Consultant^{CM} can only wear one hat at any given time in a case. As a CLNC® consultant you must establish up front with the attorney whether you are wearing the hat of the expert witness or the consulting expert. The question to ask the attorney is, "Am I expected to testify at any time in the future?" If the answer is "yes," or even "maybe," consider yourself a testifying expert and conduct yourself accordingly.

- The Certified Legal Nurse Consultant^{CM} should never start out as a consulting expert, only to find that she will be testifying. Services appropriate as a consulting expert might damage the case as an expert witness. Additionally, the attorney now has to find someone who is willing to testify, and the client relationship will probably suffer.

Vickie, her mentors, staff and successful CLNC® consultants all attest to the fact that she is the only person to consider when one wishes to become a successful Certified Legal Nurse Consultant^{CM}.

– Laura Wall, RN

- The Certified Legal Nurse Consultant[CM]
might begin with the understanding that she
will serve as an expert witness and shift to
being a consulting expert (e.g., if her opinion
does not comport with the opinion of the
hiring attorney, or if she honestly believes
someone else is better qualified to testify on
the matter).

Professional expertise.

- Testifying experts should be active in the
healthcare setting to lend credibility to their
opinions and to eliminate problems with
being labeled a "professional expert witness"
or "hired gun."
- Some states require that the expert was
actively practicing at the time of the incident
made the basis of the lawsuit.
- Some jurisdictions require that the expert
witness be active in the specialty implicated
to be legally qualified.
- A few states require that the testifying expert
be licensed within the state or a contiguous
state.

Discoverability.

- All nonprivileged and relevant materials
that an expert witness uses in preparing
opinions are discoverable. Any document
normally protected under attorney-client
privilege used by the testifying expert to
refresh her memory is generally held to
have waived any privilege by the attorney's
voluntary disclosure of the confidential
communication.

- The testifying expert should be very cautious about her conduct.
  - Do not discuss the case with others.
  - Do not participate heavily in liaison activities with clients and other consultants.
  - Check with the attorney before putting anything in writing.
  - Make all written reports as brief as possible.
  - Avoid basing an opinion on someone else's summary or version of the case.
- The consulting expert's work product is generally treated as the attorney's work product. The written material and mental impressions formulated by the attorney are generally protected from disclosure as the attorney's work product. The attorney's strategies, themes, assessments of the strengths and weaknesses of the case, conclusions, opinions and legal theories are afforded the highest level of protection. The fact that the consulting expert's work product is protected gives the attorney the opportunity to reject unfavorable potential testifying experts without having to disclose them to the opposition.

The protection of work product is qualified – not absolute.

- Protection extends only to "documents and tangible things," but facts contained in those documents can be discoverable.

It is refreshing to listen to a speaker who is passionate about nurses and is a strong advocate for them. We need to change the slogan that 'nurses eat their young.' Vickie is a great example of being the exact opposite.
– Lesley Atton, RN

- Protected documents must have been prepared in anticipation of litigation or for trial. "Documents prepared in the regular course of business" are not protected.
- The party seeking discovery of an attorney's work product must show substantial need and must be unable, without undue hardship, to obtain the substantial equivalent of the materials by other means.
- The protection can be waived if the attorney sharing opinion work product with an expert potentially waives protection of these materials if the attorney's intent was that the witness use the materials in forming an opinion. Some courts require disclosure to the opposition of all materials the attorney provides to the TE in anticipation of trial; therefore, protection of the attorney's work product is completely waived.
- Exceptions to the consulting expert's protection exist and the CE's opinion is discoverable if a TE considered the opinion in forming her own opinions. Federal Rules of Civil Procedure suggest that mere review opens the opinion to discovery. Certified Legal Nurse Consultants[CM] should always label reports *Confidential for Attorney-Client Use Only*. The party seeking discovery cannot obtain facts or opinions on the same subject by other means. This exception is rarely applied but can happen if the opposing party has retained the only expert on a

particular matter. Also the same inspection or examination made by one party's expert cannot be made by the opposing party's expert.

These distinctions in discoverability highlight why the attorney benefits from using both a consulting expert and testifying expert.

Scope of Practice of the CLNC® Consultant

Distinction Between Roles of the CLNC® Consultant and the Attorney

The Certified Legal Nurse Consultant^{CM} provides medical (consulting expert only) and nursing opinions as the expert on health, illness and injury and on the inner workings of the healthcare system.

The attorney is the expert on the legal issues and the law governing the case. The Certified Legal Nurse Consultant^{CM} does not render legal advice.

The attorney serves as the advocate, the person who pleads and urges the cause of another. The testifying expert should never advocate a position in the case. The consulting expert might advocate a position or do something that can be construed as advocacy but should remain objective at all times.

CLNC® Consultant's Major Role – Educator

The Certified Legal Nurse Consultant^{CM} does not speak for the patient but rather represents and speaks for the nursing profession. The patient is not the focus but can be the beneficiary of the CLNC® consultant's involvement in the case.

The Vickie Milazzo Institute system is unparalleled. I will have all the resources I need to make my business as a Certified Legal Nurse Consultant^{CM} successful.
– Diane Ehrig, RN

The Certified Legal Nurse Consultant^{CM} educates:

- Attorney-clients.
- Opposing attorneys.
- Jurors.
- Plaintiffs and defendants.
- Judges.
- Resource consultants.
- Consumers.

Clients Who Use CLNC® Services

- Attorneys (plaintiff and defense).
- Insurance companies.
- Healthcare facilities.
- Other Certified Legal Nurse Consultants^{CM}.
- Governmental agencies at all levels.
- Private corporations (e.g., for developing corporate strategies for quality assurance, risk identification and management, evaluation and control of loss exposure).

CLNC® Services

CLNC® Service	Consulting Expert	Testifying Expert
1. Screen or investigate cases for merit.	Yes	Yes
2. Define the applicable standards of care.	All disciplines	Nursing only
3. Define deviations from, and adherences to, the applicable standards of care.	All disciplines	Nursing only
4. Assess the alleged damages and/or injuries.	Yes	Nursing issues only
5. Identify factors that caused or contributed to the alleged damages and/or injuries.	Yes	Nursing issues only
6. Organize, tab and paginate medical records.	Yes	Yes
7. Summarize, translate and interpret medical records.	Yes	Yes
8. Identify and recommend potential defendants.	Yes	Yes

Vickie is such a dynamic speaker, I literally hung on most every word. Everything I read said that this was the best and most respected program. From start to finish, it appears to cover every detail.

– Janet Smith, RN

CLNC® Service	Consulting Expert	Testifying Expert
9. Conduct literature searches and integrate the literature and standards/ guidelines into the case analysis.	Yes	Only to support testimony
10. Research and analyze the validity and reliability of research studies relied on by all parties.	Yes	Yes
11. Identify and review relevant medical records, hospital policies and procedures, other essential documents and other tangible items.	Yes	Yes
12. Expand the attorney's medical library	Yes	Yes

CLNC® Service	Consulting Expert	Testifying Expert
13. Interview clients, key witnesses and experts.	Yes	No, except subsequent treating providers and life care planners
14. Consult with healthcare providers	Yes	Rarely
15. Identify types of testifying experts needed.	Yes	Yes
16. Locate and interface with expert witnesses.	Yes	Less common
17. Communicate with potential testifying experts.	Yes	No
18. Analyze and compare expert witness reports and other work products.	Yes	Yes

I selected Vickie Milazzo Institute's program because we usually judge teachers by how successful their students are.

– Irina Groys, RN

CLNC® Service	Consulting Expert	Testifying Expert
19. Serve as liaison between the attorney and healthcare providers, testifying experts, parties, witnesses and other consultants.	Yes	Rarely
20. Prepare interrogatories.	Yes	Verbally only
21. Review and draft responses to various legal documents and correspondence for the attorney's signature.	Yes	Review – yes; draft – verbally only
22. Assist in exhibit preparation.	Yes	Yes
23. Prepare deposition and trial (cross or direct) questions.	Yes	Verbally only
24. Review, analyze and summarize depositions, including past testimony.	Yes	Yes

CLNC® Service	Consulting Expert	Testifying Expert
25. Attend depositions, trials, review panels and arbitration and mediation hearings.	Yes	Only the expert's own deposition, etc.
26. Help prepare witnesses and experts for deposition and trial.	Yes	No
27. Develop written reports for use as study tools by the attorney.	Yes	Brief reports only – not study tools
28. Coordinate and attend independent medical examinations (IMEs).	Yes	Yes
29. Develop life care plans.	No	Yes
30. Coordinate and assist in facilitating focus groups and mock trials.	Yes	No

I am extremely excited. I have followed Vickie Milazzo Insitute for over ten years and have been impressed by its growth and reputation.

– Jerri Simcik, RN

The CLNC® Consultant's Impact on the Legal System

As a CLNC® consultant these specially trained RNs represent and speak for the nursing profession while upholding the standards of care for the healthcare community by:

- Identifying meritorious cases and communicating deviations from recognized standards.
- Identifying fraudulent and nonmeritorious claims and helping to defend against them or keep them out of the judicial system.
- Helping to ensure that the legal system uses scientific, medical and nursing information properly and without distortion.
- Providing a cost-effective adjunct to the litigation process.

The result of the involvement of Certified Legal Nurse Consultants[CM] is improved quality of care and the promotion of justice.

Take 5 Simple Steps to Launch Your CLNC® Career

by Vickie L. Milazzo, RN, MSN, JD

These RNs have shared their success stories with you for a reason. They are living a life they never could have imagined until they became Certified Legal Nurse Consultants^{CM}, and they want other smart, hardworking RNs like you to achieve the same success they enjoy.

If you're at a stage in your nursing career where you're ready for something different, new and exciting, I invite you to take your first easy step, today. Legal nurse consulting can be the satisfying, prosperous career you've been looking for. You are on the brink of that discovery, that success, and I share your excitement.

> *"Certified Legal Nurse Consultants^{CM} want other smart, hardworking RNs like you to achieve the same success they enjoy."*

One step at a time, you can build a CLNC® business that brings you the financial rewards you deserve.

Your secret to success can be as simple as making and keeping my 5 Promises.

There has never been a better time to become a Certified Legal Nurse Consultant℠. Of the 1,687,830* attorneys in practice today, 25% deal with medical malpractice and personal injury cases — that's more than 421,000 possible clients for you. Not to mention tens of thousands of insurance companies and HMOs that need your CLNC® services. The potential for CLNC® consultants is unlimited. I have never seen a more exciting, more vibrant, more fun time to start your legal nurse consulting practice than today.

One step at a time, you can make this happen for yourself. You can build a CLNC® business that matters, that works for you and that brings you the financial rewards you deserve.

What would your life look like if every moment of it was absolutely enriched, fulfilled and swelling with joy? Think about it — your health, relationships, career, spirituality and finances are the best they can be and you greet each day with energy and enthusiasm for whatever comes your way. What would accomplish that?

My 5 Promises Can Be the Secret to Your Success

Your secret to success can be as simple as making and keeping my 5 Promises. After all, the most important promises are the ones we make to ourselves.

---

*Reported by state bar associations to Vickie Milazzo Institute in 2014.

When I pioneered legal nurse consulting in 1982, I made 5 Promises that I've continued to make daily for more than three decades. These are not the only secrets to my success, but I know my business would not be where it is today if I hadn't kept these essential success promises. Make these promises today, and they will guide you in starting your new career as a successful Certified Legal Nurse Consultant[CM].

Promise 1
I will only work my passion.

We all know when we discover something we feel passionate about. We feel amazingly energetic. Desire is energy. Have you ever experienced a time when desire overcame all physical, emotional and intellectual barriers? Like a child waking up on Christmas morning, you spring alert full speed ahead. Why can't we experience that passion – that vitality and energy – not only on Christmas but every day? Believe me, you can.

When you wake up every day to a life and career you're passionate about, you experience maximum joy. Now is the time to turn on your passion for legal nurse consulting. Don't wait another day.

Promise 2
I will go for it or reject it outright.

If you want something better for your life and career, you owe it to yourself to go for it or reject it outright. Don't leave the dream dangling as a reminder of what you don't have the time, courage or enthusiasm to grab. Do it or forget it. If you want to become

When you wake up every day to a life and career you're passionate about, you experience maximum joy.

If you want something better for your life and career, you owe it to yourself to go for it or reject it outright.

a CLNC® consultant, don't wait for the conditions in your life to be perfect. That will never happen.

One thing that helps me overcome my career fears is perspective. Think about the worst thing that could happen if you go for it. Unless it's worse than cancer, I say, "What have I got to lose?"

It's perfectly okay to admit that a commitment is not right for you and to reject it outright. After all, this is your life, your passionate future. What's not okay is to hold back and put less than everything into a commitment that is your passion.

I have a fear of cliff-hanging heights. Despite that fear, I stepped out of an airplane at 14,000 feet to skydive. Once out of the plane, I couldn't step back in. I was truly committed. Make that kind of all-or-nothing commitment to your own career choice and you'll wake up each day to a career you love.

Promise 3
*I will take one action step a day
toward my career goals.*

Dreams and visions are great, but without action they are nothing more than hallucinations. Without action your visions scud away and dissolve like clouds. I've met many people much smarter than I am who had dreams and ideas but didn't do anything with them. They didn't take action.

I created a new profession and led thousands of nurses to success. I accomplished that goal with *one action step at a time.* I had to take action every day to build the momentum necessary to live my career dreams. By taking action every day you

Think about the worst thing that could happen if you go for it. Unless it's worse than cancer, I say, 'What have I got to lose?'

develop the habit and discipline to make your vision a reality.

Where you focus is where you will yield results. When you focus not just on the idea but on making it happen, you stay in motion, not just dreaming your passions but living them.

If you want big results, you must guard your time carefully and focus on Big Things. Every day, take at least one action step on the Big Thing that brings you closer to CLNC® success.

Promise 4
I commit to being a success student for life.

Success breeds success. Becoming a success student for life is about practicing being successful. What's hard today is easy tomorrow — with practice. I've been in business for over two decades, and I still learn every day — from my students, staff members, favorite writers, speakers and successful CEOs. There are two ways to learn:

- ▶ The hard way — through trial and error, making lots of mistakes.
- ▶ The easy way — through the right mentor who has already achieved success. No matter what problem you encounter, the CLNC® Mentors and I have already successfully managed a challenge just like it.

No matter what the subject, there's always more to learn. Commit now to being a lifetime student and to learning not only from your own mistakes and accomplishments but also from successful CLNC® Mentors.

Where you focus is where you will yield results....
If you want big results, you must guard your time carefully and focus on Big Things.

What's hard today is easy tomorrow.

Promise 5
I believe as a nurse I really can do anything.

Any time I have hesitated to take action toward living my dream, it was because I had stopped believing in myself. Today, when an opportunity arises and I find myself hesitating, I remember, "I am a nurse and nurses can do anything!"

Think about your ability to make split-second decisions that are the difference between life and death for your patients. Remind yourself: "If I can save lives in the middle of the night while the rest of the world is sleeping and an MD is nowhere in sight, surely I can succeed as a CLNC® consultant."

Honor yourself daily with this fact: "I am a nurse and I can do anything!"

This proven life plan works. And it's easy. Apply these 5 success promises today. I guarantee your life will become an adventure more powerful, satisfying and fun than you can imagine.

Embrace your amazing new career without limits today.

Promise BIG and promise NOW!

Vickie

Vickie L. Milazzo, RN, MSN, JD
The Pioneer of Legal Nurse Consulting

Adapted from Wicked Success Is Inside Every Woman *(published by John Wiley & Sons, Inc.), available wherever books are sold.*

> *Remind yourself: 'If I can save lives in the middle of the night while the rest of the world is sleeping and an MD is nowhere in sight, surely I can succeed as a CLNC® consultant.'*

About the *Editor*

Vickie L. Milazzo, RN, MSN, JD

nc. Top 10 Entrepreneur Vickie L. Milazzo, RN, MSN, JD is founder and president of Vickie Milazzo Institute. Vickie single-handedly pioneered the field of legal nurse consulting in 1982. According to *The New York Times*, she "crossed nursing with the law and created a new profession." Her master's degree in nursing, with a concentration in education, and her law degree uniquely qualified Vickie to invent this profitable career opportunity for RNs.

Vickie Changed the Face of Nursing

Named by *Inc.* magazine as one of the Top 5000 Fastest-Growing Private Companies in America, the Institute is the oldest and largest legal nurse consulting training institute and the only publishing company exclusively devoted to this field. Vickie created the trademark CLNC® Certification Program, the first national legal nurse consulting certification. She then built the *National Alliance of Certified Legal Nurse Consultants* (*NACLNC*®), a professional association of approximately 4,000 members. Nationally recognized by attorneys, the CLNC® Certification is the official certification of the *NACLNC*® Association.

Vickie has trained, coached and mentored more than 24,000 RNs as Certified Legal Nurse Consultants^{CM}, empowering them to take control of their lives, create exciting nursing careers and achieve financial freedom. She is recognized as the nation's expert on legal nurse consulting and as a dynamic role model by tens of thousands of nurses. Her company was named by *Inc.* magazine as one of the Top 50 Education Companies in America. Vickie teaches the innovative business strategies that changed the face of nursing and earned her a place on the national list of *Inc.* Top 10 Entrepreneurs.

New York Times Bestselling Author Defines the Standards for Legal Nurse Consulting

She is the author of the *New York Times* Bestseller, *Wicked Success Is Inside Every Woman*, published by John Wiley & Sons, *Inc.* and the *Wall Street Journal* bestseller, *Inside Every Woman: Using the 10 Strengths You Didn't Know You Had to Get the Career and Life You Want Now.*

Vickie is also the author of the national bestsellers *Core Curriculum for Legal Nurse Consulting*® textbook; the CLNC® Certification

Program; the Private and *NACLNC®* Apprenticeships; *I Am a Successful CLNC® Success Journal* and *Create Your Own Magic for CLNC® Success, Second Edition.* She is a contributor to the *Nursing Leadership Encyclopedia* and is coauthor of several books: *101 Great Ways to Improve Your Life; Rising to the Top* coauthored with Jim Rohn and Jack Canfield; and *Roadmap to Success* coauthored with Ken Blanchard and Stephen Covey. Vickie is the author of Vickie's Legal Nurse Consulting Blog at LegalNurse.com/VickiesBlog.

As the authoritative educator in her field, Vickie has been featured or profiled in numerous publications, including *The New York Times, Women's Health, Chicago Tribune, The Huffington Post, St. Louis Post-Dispatch, Houston Woman Magazine, NurseWeek, Entrepreneur, Small Business Success, Cincinnati Enquirer, Houston Chronicle, Investor's Business Daily, Pittsburgh Business Times, Ladies Home Journal, Texas Bar Journal,* Knight Ridder Media Services, *Los Angeles Times, Philadelphia Inquirer, Working Nurse, Baltimore Sun, Fort Worth Star-Telegram,* various Gannett publications and in more than 220 newspapers reaching 16.6 million readers.

Her work has been published everywhere from *USA Today* and *Seventeen* to *PINK* magazine and in many nursing, legal and business media, such as Time.com, MSNBC.com, StartupNation.com, YoungUpstarts.com, *Lawyers USA, Nursing Spectrum, Forensic Nurse, American Journal of Nursing, National Medical-Legal Reporter,*

Association of Trial Lawyers of America Newsletter and *Entrepreneur's StartUps*.

A nationally acclaimed keynote speaker and member of the National Speakers Association, Vickie has spoken for groups such as the American Association for Justice, The Oprah Winfrey Boys & Girls Club, Texas Trial Lawyers Association, Farmers Insurance, Oncology Nursing Society, eWomen Network, the Kripalu Center for Yoga and Health and other business and professional organizations.

Vickie's Nationwide Media Attention Spotlights the CLNC® Profession

Vickie has appeared on national TV, including *Fox & Friends* and *Fox Business Network* in New York City, KCAL in Los Angeles and KHOU and KRIV in Houston, as an expert on legal nurse consulting, entrepreneurship and career advancement. As a contributor to the National Public Radio program, *This I Believe®*, she shared her success strategies with NPR listeners. NPR has an audience of more than 26 million listeners. Vickie has also been featured on over 200 other national and local radio stations, reaching more than 20 million listeners, including XM Satellite Radio, Sirius Satellite Radio, KMAZ (Los Angeles), WONX (Chicago), WWAM (Philadelphia), WKNH (Boston) and WFNY (NYC). Vickie's favorite TV appearance was when she was interviewed by Aliysn Camerota on *Fox & Friends*, a national show with up to two million viewers.

Her other television appearances include ABC, CBS, FOX, NBC, *At Home Live*, Better TV (New York), *Great Day Houston*, *The CEO Show*, Bloomberg TV and dozens more.

Awards and Recognition

Vickie's many awards and honors include:

- *New York Times* Bestselling Author
- *Inc.* Top 10 Entrepreneur – one of the top 10 entrepreneurs in the U.S.
- *Inc.* Top 5000 Fastest-Growing Private Company in America
- *Inc.* Top 50 Fastest-Growing Education Company
- Stevie® Award (Business's Oscar) – Mentor of the Year
- *USA Today* Bestselling Author
- *Wall Street Journal* Bestselling Author
- *Inc.* Bestselling Business Author
- Most Innovative Small Business by Pitney Bowes®
- Top 100 Small Business in Houston
- Top 25 Woman-Owned Business in Houston
- Top 50 Fastest-Growing Woman-Owned Business in Houston
- Telly Award for Video Presentation Production
- Top 50 Most Influential Woman in Houston
- *NurseWeek* Nursing Excellence Award for Advancing the Profession

▸ Susan G. Komen's Hope Award for Ambassadorship

Vickie earned her bachelor of science in nursing at the University of St. Thomas and her master of science in nursing at Texas Woman's University, both in Houston. She earned her juris doctor at South Texas College of Law.

Mentor of the Year Transforms Careers

In all her work Vickie openly shares her practical and proven strategies as she coaches and mentors nurses to take charge of their professional destiny. Vickie is a powerful advocate for women in business and for nurses. Her vision is to revolutionize nursing careers one RN at a time. Her audiences are transformed and inspired to action by her extensive business expertise, irresistible drive and vibrant energy. The most common refrain from nurses attending her programs is, *"She changed my life!"*